meditation 24/7

Also by Camille Maurine and Lorin Roche:

Meditation Secrets for Women

Other books by Lorin Roche, Ph.D.:

Meditation Made Easy

Whole Body Meditations

Breath Taking

meditation 24/7

PRACTICES TO ENLIGHTEN
EVERY MOMENT OF THE DAY

CAMILLE MAURINE and LORIN ROCHE, Ph.D.

Andrews McMeel Publishing

Kansas City

 For information, write Andrews McMeel Publishing, an Andrews McMeel Universal company, 4520 Main Street, Kansas City, Missouri 64111.

04 05 06 07 08 TWP 10 9 8 7 6 5 4 3 2 1

ISBN: 0-7404-4715-0

Library of Congress Control Number: 2004102779

Book design by Desiree Mueller

Dedicated to all those throughout the ages
who have kept alive the wisdom of
enlightenment in everyday life

Contents

INTRODUCTION

Meditation 24/7 is a guide for waking up to the richness of your life. We offer these practices to remind you how attainable and close at hand this awareness can be.

Much of the great stuff in life is really simple. Hidden inside your most mundane moments are pathways to heightened and enlightened appreciation. Consider, for example:

- Awakening from a deep sleep and lingering in that blissful state before getting up
- Drinking your morning tea or coffee with intense pleasure, as if it were an elixir of life
- Hugging someone you love with fervor, as you would after a long separation, even if it's been only a few hours
- Walking and feeling the joy of movement as you stride along
- Eating a simple meal and taking great delight in each bite
- Being aware of all the people you love, and feeling your heart melt into openness
- Lying down, giving in to the heaviness of fatigue, and relaxing so deeply that in a few minutes you are rested and ready for action

These experiences are accessible to anyone, in the course of an ordinary day. When we take an ordinary moment and pay extraordinary attention, magic happens. It's these magical moments that create a vibrant and meaningful life.

Although they often flash by without being appreciated, these moment-by-moment happenings make up the texture of our lives. If we miss too many of them because we're distracted, fatigued, or stressed, later we may feel that we have missed out on our real life.

Extraordinary attention can be cultivated. We can learn to be open to what life is offering. When we practice giving full attention to the motions of life, this is meditation. In this book, we present fourteen meditations that you can do at transitional moments throughout your day. You don't have to go anywhere, or change yourself at all. You can start right here and now.

WHAT IS MEDITATION?

Since the dawn of time, people have been awakening to the joy and beauty of life, while moving through their everyday activities. Sometimes they talked about these enlightening experiences, or made songs or paintings about them. What we now know of meditative techniques is rooted in thousands of years of people sharing knowledge about how to cultivate the wisdom that comes from within.

Meditation is the human instinct to savor life's beauty and wonder. This has great survival value because it trains us to be alert, aware of our surroundings, at ease, and intimately connected with ourselves and others, all at the same time.

You might be surprised to hear that meditation is a built-in ability we all have. But it's true, and you can do it, because the capacity to meditate is right there in your responsiveness to life. If you sit down, close your eyes, and pay attention to your breath in a restful way, you'll be meditating.

Life is full of tiny pleasures: the feel of the sun on your cheeks; the sound of the wind; the color of the sky and trees; the expressions on the faces of the people around you; the smells of food cooking; the sensation in your heart when you see someone you love coming toward you. If you pause in the midst of any such experience, and give yourself over to appreciating it fully, you are entering the realm of meditation.

When you meditate, you can take pleasure in all of your senses—touch, hearing, vision, smell, taste, and even your sense of balance. The more senses you use, the merrier—the more interesting and engaging meditation will feel. It's okay to enjoy it immensely.

Think of meditation as the practice of falling in love with life. In love, we pay attention with heightened appreciation. We are open to experience and our heart is moved. Meditation is the process of intentionally cultivating our capacity to pay attention in this exquisite way. All the disciplines and techniques of meditation amount to cultivating what we do naturally when we are in love.

To practice meditation, select some quality of life you love, and attend to it tenderly, gently, and restfully. When you love someone or something, you want to hang out, be with that person or thing, and give and receive appreciation. You want to be in the flow of give-and-take. Meditation is the restful, inward, accepting part of the give-and-take of love. The key to meditation is that you set things up so you are restful. When you rest in loving attentiveness, the vibrating silence that's underneath outer activity can emerge.

You can meditate on the simplest aspect of life, such as a breath. Each breath can seem like a great gift, the universe itself flowing into you and giving you life. When you do this, it is as if you draw energy out of each breath and each sensation, and any fatigue just drops away. In the space of a few minutes you are refreshed and ready to engage fully with life again.

Breath is, after all, one of the main ways that life is renewed in your body, moment to moment. You should be delighted that you are breathing. Spiritual people the world over say that breath is a gift from God, an immediate, ongoing, free gift of the Holy Spirit. Each breath of air you take is created by the entire ecosystem on Earth, including all the trees, plants in the oceans, and the sun, which provides the energy for photosynthesis. Biologically speaking, breath is a gift from the whole world, the solar system, and all of creation.

Right now, for example, start to pay attention to the feeling of the breath flowing in through your nose, going down into your chest and belly, and then turning to flow out again. Exhale with a quiet whoosh or soft sigh. Continue for ten or fifteen breaths, which is about a minute. You are on your way.

WHO MEDITATES?

As you are reading this book, people all over the world are using meditation techniques to prepare to be at their best. Athletes, surgeons, dancers, actors, martial artists, and business executives are meditating so that they will be able to perform with excellence under pressure.

Singers are meditating to tune their voices and bodies so they can sing more passionately and without stress. Mothers to be are meditating in preparation for giving birth. Trackers are meditating to be at one with nature. Taoist, Buddhist, Hindu, and Christian monks are doing long meditations as part of their life of devotion. And regular people with jobs and families are meditating for a few minutes in the morning and evening as a way of caring for themselves, releasing stress and fatigue, and remembering the Big Picture of their lives. In addition, people in therapy are meditating as part of their healing process. Members of AA (Alcoholics Anonymous) and other 12-step programs are doing the eleventh step, which is prayer and meditation.

There are formal, intentional situations where meditation techniques are practiced, and there are also many informal situations in which people slip into meditation spontaneously. Lovers sitting and holding hands, just being together, can enter a meditative state. People gazing at sunrises and sunsets can drift into a peaceful reverie.

Wildlife photographers, sitting still for hours waiting for animals to appear, can meditate spontaneously. People waking up in the middle of the night, worried about their kids, friends, spouses, or themselves, can let go, slip into a meditative state, find peace, and eventually fall asleep. In churches, temples, and homes, people slip into meditation while saying their prayers.

Right now, there are people sitting by rivers and oceans, just gazing at the flow and ripples, and entering meditation without really noticing. Somewhere on the planet, someone is sitting and looking at a fire. The flames have burned away her troubles, and she feels with every cell in her body that life is good, the heart is warm, and love can shine forth from her again, in spite of everything.

When people thrive in meditation, it's because they have learned to customize the techniques to fit their lives. When people quit, usually it's because they haven't found a way that they love. In this book, we are encouraging you to approach meditation through your own everyday moments, and to experience them with more gusto and awareness. Linger for an extra sixty seconds or even several minutes, as you make the transition from sleeping to waking, home to commuting, work to lunch break, or as you walk in the door from work. In this way, you will learn to meditate in a style that is natural for you.

WHY MEDITATE?

Meditation can help you to enjoy life more and function better. Meditating regularly enhances physical health and vitality, and promotes mental clarity. Emotionally, when you meditate you will notice a deepened awareness of your feelings, and a greater capacity to give and receive love.

Hundreds of scientific studies over the last several decades have established that meditation has significant and measurable physical, mental, and emotional benefits. Here are just a few:

Physical Benefits of Meditation

- Your muscles and nerves relax profoundly.
- You are able to rest deeply and recover quickly from fatigue.
- You have a way to release stress from your nervous system, reducing stress-related ailments.
- Your immune system becomes stronger and your body is able to heal more rapidly.
- Your blood pressure is lowered if it is high.
- You become more comfortable in your body.
- Your senses open up and come alive.
- Your ability to experience physical pleasure increases. You are a better lover, more in touch with all your senses.

These physical benefits are side effects of the mental attitude of relaxed attention you are cultivating.

Mental Benefits of Meditation

- You can see and hear your own thoughts more clearly.
- You are more alert.
- You are able to stay calmer under pressure.
- You are able to shift perspective quickly from narrow focus to big picture.
- You perceive more beauty in life.
- You have a sense of how things connect, how they work together.
- You have more choice in how you respond to the world, for example, whether to get stressed or not.
- You are more open to new experiences.
- You are more accepting of your individuality.

The physical and mental benefits of meditation affect your emotional life by bringing you into inner balance. Meditating puts you in touch with yourself and your authentic feelings as well, helping you to learn from and integrate your emotions.

Emotional Benefits of Meditation

- You learn to accept all your emotions.
- You have more empathy with others.
- You feel more connected with those you love.
- Life seems more harmonious.
- You are able to give and receive pleasure, attention, and love.
- You can more easily let go of resentment and hurt.
- You are a better friend and lover because you are able to listen more fully.
- You have better boundaries; you know where you end and another begins.
- You have a specific time and technique to feel and heal your heartaches and emotional wounds.

Spirituality can be thought of as the wholeness of our being. Meditation gives us a chance to integrate and harmonize our physical, mental, and emotional worlds. Through meditation we come into relationship with the vastness of life.

Spiritual Benefits of Meditation

- You have a sense of oneness with the world.
- You experience more wonder and awe at creation.
- You tune in to your essence, your soul.
- You are more grateful.
- You express more compassion.
- You directly experience that life is sacred.
- You feel connected with the soul of humanity. You are at home in the cosmos.
- You develop spirituality in your own way, gradually awakening to an intimate communion with life.
- You begin to come to terms with the mystery of death and birth. You feel more comfortable with things unseen.
- Your sense of the meaning of life deepens.

It is surprising that such a simple practice can have these profound benefits. This is because life is all one piece, and when you pay loving attention to the flow of life within and around you, all dimensions of your being are positively affected. Meditation is just a name we give to cultivating our best, most loving attention.

HOW DO I BEGIN?

You can begin right where you are now, in the course of your day. The meditation practices in this book are constructed around transitional moments, when you are moving from one activity to another. Just select one of the practices that appeals to you. Read the meditation, and then take a couple of minutes to explore it.

You can meditate anywhere. The physical setting doesn't have to be precious or rarefied. You don't have to be on a mountaintop, inside a cave, or in a meditation room to get the benefits. Sitting on a park bench or standing in line at the grocery store works just as well.

Some people find that meditating many times a day, for a few minutes here and there, works better than sitting for a longer period once or twice a day. These shorter sessions can be equally if not more effective because they give you regular doses of relaxed attention. You will discover for yourself how to make use of these times to center and renew yourself.

I Don't Have Time to Meditate

No matter how busy you are, there is always time for a moment to remember what you love, take a breath in appreciation, and let yourself be changed, inspired, vivified by it. You will function better after taking this moment and make up for the "lost time." It is a good thing to be able to relax and refresh yourself quickly, so you can carry on with your work in the world.

Meditation does not have to be another "chore" you gotta do, another program you can't get with. You can do meditation because you love it. A businessman once said, "I don't have time *not* to meditate. I can't afford not to function at my very best."

Here are some of the qualities that meditation is known for developing:

Clarity	Compassion	Humor	Focus
Openness	Boundaries	Power	Ease
Wisdom	Gratitude	Vitality	Inspiration
Freedom	Sensuality	Delight	Love

Chapter 1

FLOW WITH YOUR GO

Flow with Your Go

The Course of a Day

Meditation 24/7 gives you meditations to do in the flow of your day, from the moment you awaken until you fall asleep at night. Doing these awareness practices can enhance the quality of your experience in relationships, work, and play.

Every day we awaken, love, work, learn, and fall asleep. This is the fundamental rhythm of our lives. The day is structured by the many transitions we make—from sleep to waking, from solitude to socializing, from rest to work, from being out in the world to coming home again. Normally we might not pay much attention to these in-between times, but we can learn to use such mundane moments to recharge our inner batteries and refresh our outlook on life.

When we change from one mode of being or activity to another, it's good to pause, tune in to ourselves, review our priorities, and make any necessary adjustments. These mini-tune-ups throughout the day help us to meet our challenges with more clarity, creativity, and heart.

Life is increasingly complex and unpredictable. Technological upheavals, global uncertainties, and the ever-fickle marketplace challenge us all to be alert and centered within what often feels chaotic and insecure. In the midst of so much flux, we need to become more adaptable and resilient. We all want to stay afloat and move with some measure of confidence, wisdom, and grace.

In addition to the changes in the world, we each move through many personal transformations in the course of a life, and in the course of a day. There are the big transitions: the physical and emotional changes of growing up, making a living, falling in and out of love, illness, and aging. If you are in a major transition time, such as starting a new job, getting married or divorced, having children or taking care of ailing parents, or experiencing menopause or midlife, having a meditation practice will give you valuable resources to guide and sustain you. Meditation is a way of tapping into your innate and instinctive survival wisdom.

The larger life passages challenge us in obvious ways, but when we meet the little daily transitions with curiosity, we discover they are just as important. Each moment of change during the day is a chance to remember the qualities of life that you long for, and to cultivate the attitude that allows you to receive them.

Transitional moments are creative. In the gap between what was and what will be, new impulses have a chance to surface and be realized. When we enter a gap consciously, we can sense the creativity of the moment. We can choose how to respond to what life throws our way.

Meditation helps us get present, integrate our experience, let go, and be renewed. In the space of a few minutes, we start to unwind and sink into our essence. We tap in to our inner roots, reconnect with our heart's desire. Then when we emerge, we can meet the world fresh, prepared, and inspired.

Taking time to honor transitions may at first seem unrealistic or even taboo. In the breathless pace of contemporary life, we rush from task to task, always on to the next thing, pedaling as fast as we can to keep up. Despite our immense cultural riches, most people suffer from a kind of time poverty, or the feeling that there just isn't enough time or space in a day. Something's amiss; there's a longing but it's hard to name. We're beside ourselves, overwhelmed, maybe even depressed.

Meditation is a way of catching up with ourselves, and inhabiting our experience as human beings. When you meditate, your senses come alive and you awaken to life. You go from taking everything for granted to being grateful. When you pay conscious attention to the most ordinary moment, you may find yourself startled and enchanted. Simply waking up, or embracing someone close, taking a walk, enjoying a meal, or being at a party surprises and teaches you about yourself, about life, and about love.

By punctuating your ordinary activities with meditative awareness, you create continual access to the resources you need for coping with life's demands and staying true to what you want. You cultivate an ongoing connection to your deepest values. Linked together like pearls on a string or the threads of a tapestry, these creative pauses deepen the sense of your life as one meaningful whole.

Courting the Magic of a Day

A marvelous benefit of meditating throughout the day is that you become sensitive to the rhythms of the natural world. Each hour of the day has its own mystery and magic, each transition its soulful gift. Dawn, high noon, sunset, and night are nature's transition times. Our human transitions of waking, taking meals, venturing out, and coming home are attuned to these outer rhythms.

Pausing at these moments helps us develop a conscious relationship with the larger cycles of life, a sense of wonder and gratitude for our place within the whole. Life wants to be romanced, courted, and willingly invited. When you train yourself to notice, then enter these moments, you are in essence romancing the spirit of life. You are cultivating the capacity to be awake, alert, and grateful to be alive.

If you are competent at surviving, you have set up automated routines. You can perform your functions almost mindlessly—get up, go to work, come home, without really savoring life. Routines are good. For example, walking is a routine, and it would be tedious to have to reinvent how to walk each time we take a step. But everything—conversations with friends, sex, all our responses to the world—can become automatic. We can be numb to our own existence.

By contrast, when in your life have you felt truly alive? Awake and alert? Intensely grateful? When you savor a moment, even on the fly, you work your gratitude muscle. You are training yourself to appreciate and delight in life's small pleasures. You will notice that your senses open up, and you become more capable of perceiving novelty. You will find yourself looking at a familiar scene and seeing it afresh. You will gaze at your lover as if for the first time, and be smitten all over again.

The Rhythm of Life

Human beings sometimes forget that nature is not only out there but also in here, in our bodies, continually renewing us with its many healing rhythms. Meditation is a prime way to cooperate with nature's regenerative power.

The universe loves rhythm. From galaxies to electrons, everything is turning. The earth revolves around the sun, the moon revolves around the earth, and the whole solar system orbits the galactic center. The particles out of which everything is made are always oscillating.

Our planet's orbit gives us the *circa-annual* rhythm we call a year. The moon's orbit every twenty-eight or so days gives us a *moonth,* or a *circatrigintan* cycle. The earth's rotation on its axis every twenty-four hours gives us the *circadian* rhythm of alternating daylight and darkness we call a day.

Inside our bodies, everything flows in rhythms and cycles: our hearts beat, the breath pulses in and out, and the cells and molecules vibrate. We're energetic for many hours, and then we need to sleep. Even when we are at our most active, our body energy fluctuates in a ninety-minute to two-hour cycle, called an *ultradian* rhythm. In midmorning or midafternoon, for example, you may want to pause and take a break.

Nature's got rhythm—lots of rhythm. Life restores and sustains itself through such rhythms. At any moment in time, our bodies dance with all of these intersecting rhythms. Whenever we pause to experience ourselves, as in meditation, what we experience is the sum total or symphony of all these vibrations.

Take a moment to be aware of your body, then the season, the phase of the moon, the day of the week, the time of day, and where you are in your cycle of rest and action. Many instinctive processes are at work right now within you to tune and harmonize all these cycles. Our bodies thrive when we cooperate with these natural rhythms, and we can get out of balance—jet-lagged in place—when we override them.

When you meditate, you are putting yourself in rapport with the self-healing, self-renewing powers of your inner nature. You are a part of nature, even as you go about your daily life, with too little sleep, a commute, bills, all kinds of relationships, a job, maybe kids, parents, friends, spouses, maybe ex-spouses, plans, dreams, desires, worries, loves, fears, interests. Your craving to take a vacation or to meditate is just as much a natural instinct as the bird's urge to migrate to South America or the whale's going up and down the coast.

The wisdom of nature is always and everywhere evident, one of those obvious miracles right under our noses, inside our skin, and coursing through our veins. With every breath and heartbeat, we enact our dependence on the larger natural world. Our vital interconnectedness with the whole of life is awesome, humbling, inspiring, and enlivening. Seize the opportunity of meditation to be transformed by this awareness.

CHAPTER 2

PRACTICES

PRACTICES

These meditations are designed to be done at certain periods around the clock, but feel free to adapt them to your own schedule. Start anywhere you want, and add others when you are ready.

Many of the practices can be done whenever you like. Move It, for example, is placed in midmorning, but you can do it anytime you are walking or exercising. Likewise, the Feast Your Senses practice is featured at lunchtime, but of course it applies to breakfast and dinner as well.

When doing these meditations, take a casual, explorative attitude. Be curious, play with the practices, and find out how they can work best for you. Experiment with the length of time. Once you get the gist of a practice, you can feel the benefit in a minute or two. Conversely, you may find meditations that you love so much you want to extend them to a full twenty minutes. And then again, sometimes you may want to do only a part of the practice. There are no rules. Well, maybe one: enjoy yourself.

Some days you might even drift off to sleep during a meditation and wake up very refreshed a few minutes later. If you get so tired that you fall asleep instantly, your brain will do its best to sort through your experience while you are asleep, through dreaming.

Have the general intention to accept your experience each day. Everyone is different, and every day is different. This means that each time you do a practice, your needs will lead you in a different direction and to new discoveries.

You will have a learning curve unlike anyone else's. You may take to a meditation instantly and require very little instruction other than to give yourself the space to do it. Or you may want to take just one tiny step at a time.

Whatever your experience, call it a win. If you spend one minute just feeling yourself, good—that is a victory. If you fall asleep, good—you needed the rest. If you get absorbed in the process and attain enlightenment, that's okay, too.

Using the CD with the Book

The practices on the CD have been edited for listening and are usually shorter than what's in the book. It's a good idea to read the essay and procedure at least once before doing a meditation for the first time. Doing so will give you a chance to familiarize yourself with the whole practice and sense the meaning it might have for you.

Listening to the meditations on the CD allows you to turn your attention inward more easily. You don't have to use your hands or eyes and can simply relax into the experience. Depending on the meditation, you can listen in bed, in your living room, as a passenger in a car, plane, bus, or train, outside in nature, or even in a store or restaurant.

Most CD players can be programmed to play the tracks you want, so that you don't have to worry about turning the player off. This feature will be especially helpful with the Fall into Sleep and Still of the Night meditations. Also, if you decide to extend a meditation, you can simply let the CD stop as you continue.

Welcoming Yourself

Whenever you approach any of these meditations, take the attitude, *I welcome all parts of myself. I welcome all of who I am into this space.*

When you meditate, it is like returning home, or seeing a friend after a long absence. You will spend a while just catching up with yourself. Anything you haven't had time to feel—all the grief, anger, tension, fear, and also love, joy, and laughter—may come up. This is a healthy process. Whatever emotions come up, demanding to be felt, are already there inside you. Do not fear these experiences; learn to embrace them.

When you get quiet, you can hear the voice of your heart. You may be surprised by the intensity of your feelings. Meditating is sometimes almost like having a near-death experience, in which your whole life flashes before your eyes. You become aware of unfinished business—longings unfulfilled, actions you regret, communications left unshared. You feel the disparity between your heart's desire and what you have manifested so far.

A man came by recently on a doctor's referral to learn to meditate because he was having anxiety attacks and sleep disturbances. He has a great job, a wife who adores him, and three healthy young children. He even has a short, ten-minute commute. He has so much, he's afraid he will lose it somehow. When he came in, he said, "Whenever I get quiet, my mind is flooded with anxious thoughts. I try to push them out, but they keep coming back."

We did the Coming Home practice described on page 91, and he immediately settled into deep relaxation and restfulness. He called after a few days and said, "Whenever I meditate, I have to wade through all those thoughts zooming around in my head. That takes a couple of minutes, which seems eternal. But then, if I just breathe with the thoughts, the anxiety and fear dissolve and turn into an equally powerful gratitude. When I lie down and let go into gravity, it's as if thousands of tiny hands are holding me up. I don't have to hold it all together. The thing is, my life is so great it scares me. My great-grandparents were killed in wars or starved to death. My parents immigrated to this country and struggled for decades. What did I do to deserve all this good fortune?"

A few weeks of meditation broke the pattern that was disturbing his sleep. What he needed was to welcome his anxiety and also his gratitude. Honoring these opposites allowed him to come home to his own heart.

You never know what you are going to get when you open the door to your inner self. Your most tender longings are right there, as is the depth of your love and your fear of feeling so much. All of us have some version of fear, ways in which we hide from the immensity and intensity of love. We need a space and time to let love gently transform our fears into excitement about life.

Meditation allows you a sense of relaxation underneath the excitement, a restfulness that supports and energizes you. In any given moment, you will feel the interplay of different desires—for example, the urge to jump up and take action, to go out and use your talents, along with the craving to rest, to give in to the fatigue that comes from using your nerves and muscles. You may long for more adventure, and simultaneously long for security.

This is the nature of meditation. It is through the play of these apparent opposites that your nervous system comes into balance and integration. There is a saying, "Opposites attract." They even love each other. Meditation is the quality of attention that allows your inner opposites to come into relationship and work toward consummating a marriage. Here are a few pairs of opposites you may experience:

Quiet	❂	Exhilaration
Relaxation	❂	Alertness
Serenity	❂	Electricity
Closed eyes	❂	Open senses

The peacefulness of meditation does not come from editing or trying to numb yourself out. It comes from including and embracing all of who you are.

Meditative experiences are ever-changing, total emotional symphonies that are never really repeated. Similar themes may come back again and again, but what happens moment to moment is always varied. The essential skill of meditation is accepting and cooperating with this process. Inner peace, it turns out, takes some getting used to! So when you are exploring these practices, remember these guidelines:

- Welcome your yearning and longing.
- Welcome your worries and woes.
- Welcome your plans.
- Welcome your pains and fatigue.
- Welcome your jumpiness and speedy thoughts.
- Welcome any anger or hurt you feel.
- Welcome relaxation.
- Welcome falling asleep if that happens.

CHAPTER 3

MORNING MEDITATIONS

Morning Meditations

As nature makes the transition from darkness to light, stars, dreams, and the veiled realities of night fade into the illumination of day. The sun rises, creatures great and small begin to stir, and the life energy inside each of us swells into activity and engagement.

Morning is the youth of a day, a time of freshness and possibility. Each day offers us a clean slate, a new canvas for creativity, collaboration, and love. Morning meditations prepare us to meet the day's adventures, and to be receptive to its many gifts.

Before leaving the sanctuary of home, we can take a few moments of inner privacy to contact our essential self. We can consciously awaken to the beauty around us, remember everything that is important to us, all our loved ones, our desires and dreams. We can put ourselves into rapport with the invisible, generative powers of life.

In midmorning we can pause again in the midst of activity, tune in to our bodies, free up our energy, and refresh our minds to focus on the tasks at hand.

Even a little tuning in the morning can brighten the rest of your day.

Awakening

The transition from being asleep to being awake is one of life's little mysteries. We emerge from the fertile darkness of night and dreams, and are reborn to the light of day. These first moments of consciousness are precious: as we awaken, we create ourselves and our relationship to the world anew.

When we fall asleep, consciousness is released from the body and stretches out into the vastness of the cosmos. During the night, we surrender our bodies and psyches to the deep, healing waters of sleep. We release our grip on identity and give over to nature. We dream, drifting through an ocean of images, emotions, and movement largely beyond our control. Awakening in the morning, we return as if from another world. Awareness condenses and localizes again in the body, in this bed, this room, and this place on the planet. We come back to the particulars of our lives: all our relations, and the many ways we're engaged with the world.

Becoming aware of this transition is a potent meditation. Instead of leaping out of bed, pause for a few moments to savor what it is to awaken. Lingering in this in-between state is very interesting and even blissful. Give yourself time to bask in the miracle: *I am alive.*

The phenomenon of consciousness, that humans can be aware of our own existence, is truly a marvel. Contemplating the mystery of life, and death, is also the foundation of every spiritual tradition. Awareness of the ephemeral nature of our lives startles us out of complacency and into the present. Each moment becomes a gift, drenched in poignancy and awe. We awaken.

How you experience awakening is individual to you and can vary from day to day. The aspects of life that you cherish—the beauty you love, your sense of awe and wonder—are your guides. Your practice is the deepening, unfolding discovery of what this means to you.

Prolonging and exploring these first moments in the morning sets the tone for the entire daylight journey to come. Instead of "getting up on the wrong side of the bed," take the time to establish the quality of experience you crave. Improve your percentage of "right side" awareness—gratitude for the gift of life.

Awakening Practice

When: *Before rising in the morning*

Where: *In bed*

Position: *Lying down*

Time: *5 to 10 minutes*

Whenever possible, awaken naturally without an alarm. On those days that you need to keep track of time, though, we suggest you choose a sound that is not "alarming"—a gentle gong or chime, or music of your choice. The CD will guide you, but you may also want to set three separate alarms: one to wake you up, another to go off at five or ten minutes, and time permitting, a third at twenty minutes. In this way you can gently awaken, let go and luxuriate without worrying about being late.

Drifting gently awake, gradually emerging from the world of sleep and dreams, take your time to savor the moment. When you first become aware that you are awake, do not move or open your eyes. Simply welcome the first moments of consciousness. Explore what it is to awaken.

Take a moment to allow any dreams to float into your awareness. What images linger at the fringe between the worlds of night and day? What moods or impressions remain from your nighttime journey?

Now notice the bodily experience of awakening to the day. As consciousness returns from the vastness, it gradually condenses back into your body. You become aware of being in bed, in this room, in this particular place on planet Earth. You are here. You are alive.

You are breathing. Gentle waves of breath awaken you to life, calling you into your body. Sense your body weight resting easily, the comfort of being secure in your nest. Feel how your shape snuggles into the bed. Enjoy the texture of the pillow and covers, any warmth or coolness on your skin. Receive the pleasure of this simple, relaxed state.

When you are ready to, very slowly open your eyes to the light or darkness. Cherish being awake to the light. Luxuriate in this particular quality of light. Welcome the light. Turn your attention to the source of light, the sun rising in the east, illuminating our beautiful planet. Take several breaths in appreciation.

After a few minutes, the tone of your awareness will change and become more action-oriented. You will have thoughts of the day to come, of a relationship that needs attention, or of your schedule of tasks. You'll notice your breath becoming more active as well.

At that point find your way into a morning stretch and yawn. Just as dogs and cats do when they awaken, and before they get up, stretch your animal body. Arch your back gently, extend your arms over your head, reach your legs out, breathe deeply, and enjoy the sense of movement for a minute or two.

Be aware of everyone in your life, all your loved ones,

everything that is important to you today. If you have a bedmate, give your partner a loving touch for a few moments before getting up. Reestablish your connection with a kiss, caress, or playful pat.

Now preparing to rise, imagine being in the world with the quality of awareness you desire. When you're ready, slowly curl up to a sitting position and place your feet on the ground. Sense the support of the earth beneath you, and flow up into a standing position. With another conscious breath, take in the fullness of this moment of life. Then move on into your day.

Intention:

I am grateful to be alive. I am awake to the beauty of life.

Fill Your Cup

In this meditation you treat your regular morning cup of tea or coffee as an elixir of vitality. As you drink, consciously appreciate that you are imbibing strength and nourishment from the beneficent forces of life. You fill the cup of your awareness, and the vessel of your body, with life-affirming energy and sustenance. The natural elements are always feeding and supporting us, whether we are aware of them or not. Here we consciously say yes and allow ourselves to receive.

The beginning of the day, before you launch into action, is a prime time to cultivate receptive awareness. After rising from sleep and doing whatever ablutions are necessary, settle into a chair or sofa with your favorite cup of tea, coffee, juice, water, or other beverage.

Drinking a delicious and refreshing liquid is not only sensually satisfying but also symbolic of taking in the waters of life. Without water we would not be alive. As you relish the smell, flavor, and warmth or coolness of your chosen drink, you are awakening your senses to pleasure. Simultaneously, with each sip you renew your gratitude for existence.

When you enter a receptive state, something inside lets go and spreads out. Like leaves of a tree soaking up sunlight and rain, or roots in the fertile earth, you open up to drink in the juice of life.

This opening up is not only metaphoric but also a subtle physical effect that can be sensed. In conscious relaxation, blood vessels dilate, the brain makes new connections, and all the senses become heightened. You feel peaceful, resourceful, and in rapport with the forces of life.

We are always interchanging substance with the environment. The most essential exchange happens about sixteen times a minute, more than twenty thousand times a day, and is called breathing. Conscious breathing is rapturous, yet usually we are not cognizant of breath unless something is wrong. With every inhalation, we draw in the oxygen exhaled by the flora of Earth; with every exhalation, we give back the carbon dioxide that they in turn use as food. Each breath fills your cup with the life-giving elixir of air. Awareness of this vital interdependence is an enlightenment in itself.

When we give ourselves over to the rich experience of receiving, a new world opens up. Starting your day with this meditation is like eating breakfast, the most important meal of the day.

Fill Your Cup Practice

When: *While drinking your morning beverage*

Where: *A spot that feels safe, peaceful, inspiring, soothing, or beautiful. If possible, sit where you can see trees outside.*

Position: *Sitting comfortably in a relaxed attitude. You can place your feet on the floor or curl your legs up—whatever is most natural to you.*

Time: *5 to 10 minutes.*

In this meditation, enjoy your regular morning tea, juice, or coffee with an extra bit of awareness.

Get comfortable, holding your cup. Notice its shape and weight, its temperature against the skin of your hands.

Bring the cup closer to your face. Inhale the scent for a couple of breaths. Notice that even the smell can be nourishing and stimulating. If the liquid is warm, you will be able to feel steam rising as you inhale.

Take a few sips, savoring. See how much pleasure you can take in the aroma and taste. Hold the liquid for a second in your mouth. Let it roll around your tongue before swallowing. As you drink, notice the sensations of gratitude in your body and heart.

Give yourself great leisure. Sip and pause, then take another sip.

As you continue drinking, sense the symbolism of taking in this liquid. You are receiving life-sustaining elements into your body and heart. Now think about the day ahead. What quality of energy do you need today? What kind of alertness do you want to manifest?

Choose a word, such as love, peace, harmony, power, wisdom, clarity, joy, or balance.

Breathe with your word. Meditate on its essence.

Hold your cup in your hands and say your focus word softly. Your word has a particular physical and emotional tone. With every sip, imagine you are drinking in that quality.

The energy of your word begins to vibrate within your body. As the liquid flows past your lips and tongue into your body, receive.

When you have finished drinking, place the cup down and simply breathe. Let the feeling of drinking come into your breath. Draw in the breath like an elixir, a delicious, life-giving substance. Breathe in leisurely, enjoying the energy. Then whisper your word once or twice, listening as you exhale.

If you like, open your hands so your palms face upward. This is a gesture of receiving. You are receiving from life, from the vastness of the atmosphere, the quality of energy you need for the day.

Surrender to the sensations as your body opens to be filled with this essence. Soak it up into every cell. Imagine the substance of what you desire becoming part of your flesh, circulating in your blood and breath.

Let the cup of your body be filled with vital energy.

Let the cup of your heart be filled with love.

Let the cup of your awareness be filled with gratitude for being alive.

Throughout the day, whenever you drink, whenever you are aware of breathing, know that you are receiving from the generous forces of life.

Now, gradually begin to make a transition, getting ready for breakfast. As you eat, receive the nourishment and enjoy!

Intention:

I receive from the elements of life. I give thanks for every breath.

Groom and Zoom

Grooming ourselves in the morning gives us a chance to cultivate body awareness and acceptance. If we are overly focused on our appearance, or rushing to get ready, it's easy to treat ourselves like objects. We tend to poke and prod ourselves mechanically, with no connection to our own sensuality. Men and women alike can benefit from bringing more care and consciousness to the actions of grooming.

Our culture's understanding of the body is fixated on outer image and abstract ideals of perfection. There is little appreciation of individuality, or celebration of each unique form. It takes some resolve to free yourself from these false idols.

You can learn to value, sense, and celebrate your body. Your real body is not the one in the mirror. Your real body is the rich world of sensations, movement, and energy flowing inside you. It's the way that life force is moving through you moment to moment. It's how you perceive and appreciate life, your sense of being alive.

Taking pride in lookin' good is healthy and fun. But when we lose contact with our inner body, no amount of outer approval can provide the satisfaction we seek. Even if a friend says, "Hey, you look great!" we don't believe it unless we feel great inside.

This meditation is about how you contact yourself while

preparing to greet the world. It's about bringing more awareness to your morning routine of getting showered and dressed. Through these simple practices, you can develop more joy and ease in your physical self.

Groom and Zoom Practice

When: *While bathing and getting dressed*

Where: *The bathroom*

Time: *3 to 5 minutes*

Choose pleasing bath products as a self-caring signal to your body. Find soap, shampoo, lotions, or aftershave with fragrances that you love. Have a towel that is a size, weight, softness, and color that make you happy. Minimize your use of the mirror; instead, focus on body sensations.

Taking a shower and getting dressed is a transition between your home self and your worldly self. You spruce yourself up to meet your community. When you bring sensory awareness to this preparation, you can instill dignity, pleasure, and confidence in your bodily presence.

Every immersion in water has a resonance with baptism, a mini-ritual of cleansing and renewal. After removing your clothes and before entering the shower, stand for a moment au naturel. Just as in waking this morning you were birthed to a new day, in showering you are preparing yourself to be open to new experiences today. Imagine that your nakedness right now is symbolic of this openness and newness.

Being naked, sometimes even when you're alone, can feel vulnerable and exposed, as though you've stripped not only your clothing but your veneer of personality. If you are tempted to judge your outer shape, take a deep breath and invite yourself into a new experience of your body.

Turn on the water, finding just the right warmth and pressure. As you get in the shower, enjoy the pleasurable sensation of water dancing on your skin. Feel in detail the temperature and the firmness or gentleness of water pressure. As you lather up, savor the fragrance of your shampoo or soap. Smooth the suds over your skin, feeling the silky texture as you wash or shave. Sense the movement of your hands flowing over the curves of your body.

Drying off, rub your body gently but briskly with the towel to stimulate your skin. If you use lotion, pay special attention to the quality of touch with which you apply it. Savor its smoothness and fragrance, breathing in with enjoyment.

Love your body up as you contact every part. Where would you be without it? Say a fond hello and thanks to your hands and arms, your legs and feet, your hips and haunches, for enabling you to move around and touch the world. Fondly touch your belly, breasts, or hairy chest in gratitude, for housing the tender, vital organs that keep you alive—your heart, digestive, and reproductive centers. Caress your throat and face, appreciating how they have weathered the storms of life and persevered.

Breathe in deeply, acknowledging the uniqueness of your whole body experience, all the loving and longing you have known, all that has shaped you inside and out. No one else's body has undergone the same challenges; no one but you has gleaned the exact lessons you have learned. Endorse your body for the adventures you have had, and for those that are yet to come.

Keep affirming your individuality. I am unique: this nose, this hair, these eyes. I am not a clone. Dare to celebrate your own existence.

Now, how do you want to clothe this lovable, one-of-a-kind body today? With what colors and textures do you want to adorn yourself? What costume suits your attitude, and the adventures of your day?

Begin to make the transition from your private body to your public self. As you dress and go about your business, remember your real body underneath all your outer activity.

Intention:

As I prepare to meet the world, I am in my real body. I take pleasure in my existence.

THE ROLES WE PLAY

Every transition is a chance to master the art of change. As we move through the day, many qualities are required from us. When we go from activity to activity, a range of talents is called forth. Each talent, each skill, has a personality of its own, and any individual is a unique mixture of these characters.

Outwardly, we might play the part of lover, parent, friend, executive, accountant, mediator, manager, cook, chauffeur, or gracious host. Inwardly, we may also be artist, priestess, dreamer, warrior, monk, lone wolf, wildwoman or man. Patient and healer, city dweller and nature buff, party animal and solitary traveler in the cosmos—all can coexist in one human being.

We get into trouble when we get caught up in the whirlwind and lose track of what is being called for in each situation. Think what happens when you're inappropriately acting like the boss when it's the lover who is being asked for, being the manager when you really need to dream, or being too dreamy when you need to be alert and focused on the practical.

Pausing in the transitions lets you evaluate the moment, come back to yourself, find the resource appropriate to the situation, and shift into that inner part.

The purpose of meditation is always to enhance your skills in action. Even a little meditation helps lubricate your gears and sharpen your focus. When you start meditating, you will find that you become more adaptable and resilient, and able to shift fluidly as needed.

Good to Go

Here's a quickie you can do to enhance your vitality and strengthen your boundaries. This is a good practice to do before going out the door in the morning, crossing any threshold, or whenever you want to get yourself together and be at your best.

In essence what you do with the Good to Go technique is stand somewhere and, for that moment, claim your place on earth. Take a stand there, on that spot, and let your energy spread out around you. Consciously inhabit your personal space—it's as simple as that.

All living things have boundaries. Cells have membranes; our internal organs are surrounded by fascia; the body itself has skin. Extending out from the skin for a couple of feet in all directions is a biomagnetic field, sometimes called the aura. This force field is generated by the electrical and magnetic currents in your body interacting with those of the planet. It is one of the signs that you are alive.

You can sense your magnetic field if you move your hands slowly in the space around your body. Intrusions into this energy boundary can also be physically sensed, such as the edginess you feel when someone comes too close for comfort. Conversely, when you are intimate with someone, you willingly invite her or him into your personal space.

Having a strong and appropriate energy boundary is healthful and protective, the way having a well-functioning immune system is. When your magnetic field is strong, it filters out some of the static and stress that come at you.

You can create a healthier energy field by developing awareness of the space around you. Wherever you are located, your body is related to the sky, the ground, the space behind you and to each side, as well as the space directly in front of you. You are always being enveloped and supported by space.

Good to Go is a great routine to do before going out in the world. Consider this your private "All systems go" and "Shields up!" space ritual.

Good to Go Practice

When: *Before going out the door in the morning, or any time*

Where: *Near the threshold between your home and the outer world*

Position: *Standing*

Time: *1 to 3 minutes*

Stand with your feet apart, in such a way that you have a secure foundation. Slightly soften your knees so that they are not locked.

Become aware of the ground beneath your feet, the vast body of the earth that supports you. Send your consciousness down into the ground, like roots of a tree.

Now become aware of the space above your head. Lightly touch the top of your head, then reach your hands up high, saluting the sky, the sun, and the stars.

Sweep your arms down, then bring your fingertips to your heart for a breath or two. Now release your hands forward, then out to each side, spreading them in a wide embrace. Imagine that you are claiming the space to both your left and your right.

Twist gently to each side, swinging your arms slowly to reach behind you. Extend your awareness to the area behind you and around your back. Greet the space all around you, 360 degrees.

Bring your hands to the backs of your hips, then slide them around to your belly. Feel the power of your solar plexus, belly, and pelvic center. Now release your hands and swirl them around your lower body, claiming the area all around your pelvis and legs.

Stand tall. Shift your weight from one foot to the other a couple of times, once again establishing your connection to the earth. Move your arms in every direction, saluting the space. Give thanks to the natural forces of life that surround and permeate you.

If you want, say this mantra out loud or silently:

Peace above me.
Peace below me.
Peace in front of me.
Peace behind me.
Peace all around me.

Visualize luminous energy encircling your body, like a spherical or egg-shaped force field. Imagine the whole area around you vivified by your presence, vibrating and pulsating with energy. Inside of that protective atmosphere, you are safe, relaxed, and alert.

Space itself is welcoming your fullness. Your energy is free to become as big as it wants to be, without any effort.

Take a couple of conscious breaths as a transition. Now prepare to cross the threshold into your next activity. You are good to go!

Intention:

I am present and centered in space. I am open to benevolent contact and protected from harm.

Move It

This moving meditation is an excellent midmorning refresher. You know that time, in the middle of the morning, when you feel an energy drop. All of a sudden you become aware of your bodily needs: you're thirsty, lonely, hungry, restless, and you need to go to the bathroom. This is an ultradian rhythm, one of those ninety-minute to two-hour cycles when your bodymind system calls out for maintenance.

In the middle of the morning's project, errands, or chores, give yourself a break to stretch, breathe, and move. Particularly if you have been sitting at the computer, in a meeting, or otherwise intensely focused, it's good to release physically whatever tensions have accumulated in your body or head.

Move It is a helpful practice to do when you are changing from one situation to another in which you have to play a different role. As you are about to cross that threshold, especially if the stakes are high, you will observe particular sensations and emotions. On the way to your next event, walk with excitement, frustration, anxiety, joy, or inspiration—whatever is percolating inside you. Let the movement vitalize and clear you. Then as you approach, rehearse for your new role by incorporating that tone into your walk. Move and breathe with clarity, ferocity, tenderness, or grace.

You can bring this same expressiveness into your favorite workout. First of all, it is important to find exercise you really take pleasure in, not a tedious discipline. When you discover a way of moving that you love, you want to do it and want to pay attention. Walking, running, swimming, yoga, or dancing can seem like a treat, an indulgence, a shameless delight. You can take wild joy in being a healthy animal.

Exercise of any kind can be a celebration of liveliness—the miracle of life, the miracle of having a body, the fact of being able to move at all. You can be grateful for all the processes that contribute to health. Appreciate the cleansing, nourishing flow of breath as you exercise. While you are strengthening your bones and muscles, you are oxygenating all your cells, organs, and skin. The force of life is pulsing through you everywhere.

All parts of the brain are awakened when you move your body with expressive and sensory awareness. Left and right hemispheres dance with each other, communicate, and synchronize.

There is a great deal of difference between running on autopilot and engaging all your senses with curiosity and appreciation. Consciously appreciating your bodily experience gives you what we call *kinaesthetic* awareness—perceiving the poetry and art of your motion.

Bringing this aesthetic appreciation to any kind of movement has a significant integrating effect on body, heart, and mind. You are in harmony with yourself and your environment. A sense of being alive, of being a creature of nature, and the emotional richness of experience all instill gratitude for the wonder and beauty of life.

Move It Practice

When: *Midmorning or any time between activities. Also good when exercising.*

Where: *Anywhere—office, studio, living room, in the hall, outdoors*

Position: *Standing and walking*

Time: *5 to 10 minutes*

Tune in to your body sensations. Scan your body from head to toe, noticing your mood, any tightness in your muscles or buzzing in your nerves. Just pay attention to the sensations without trying to change them in any way.

Now stretch for a few breaths. Reach your arms up high and breathe deeply. Bend your knees and curl gently down, dangling your head and hands toward the ground. Keeping your knees bent, slowly curl your back up into a standing position. Repeat this a couple of times, saluting the sky and earth.

Now put your feet in motion. Start walking, anywhere—in your room, down the hall, or outside. You can even go into the bathroom for privacy. Strut, stomp, saunter, stride, or glide.

As you walk, shake your hands with loose wrists. Sweep your arms as though you are clearing the space around you. Make sounds as you exhale, blowing out like a whale, with a "whoosh" or "whew." Play with this several times. This breath is very cleansing and energizing.

While walking, let yourself feel any irritation, discouragement, anxiety, aggression—whatever there is. Let it all come up, come to awareness, and be felt everywhere in your body as you walk. This can be uncomfortable at first.

Let the emotion come into your stride. You might not look any different to an observer, but inside you are agitated, excited, sad, or afraid. You may be quivering with fury or pacing like a caged animal. You may be powerful, dangerous, stalking in the wild like a tiger. Or perhaps you pad along meekly, cowering like a dog with its tail between its legs. Acknowledge the image and let it influence the way you walk. Express your energy, and have an attitude. Breathe out with a hiss, sigh, growl, yelp, or whimper.

As you breathe and move expressively, you are freeing yourself from the grip of constricting feelings. Give yourself some space. Imagine freedom, releasing yourself from all the demands upon you right now. Release yourself from how you have had to hold yourself together, or any way you've stopped moving. Let your energy flow with abandon.

Now just breathe and walk however you want. Open your attention to what is around you—your immediate environs, the mood of the weather outside, the quality of light from the sun or a lamp. See something you may never have noticed before—the bark of a tree, the shape of a door, the expression in someone's eyes. Hear the chatter of voices, animals, insects, birds, or machines. Pick up any scent on the wind.

Become aware of the situation you are walking toward, your next activity. What are you walking into? What kind of attention will be required? What aspect of you is going to be called forth? What do you consciously want to embody?

Breathe with the quality of awareness you want to establish: confidence, precision, patience, enthusiasm, courage, caring, support, trust. Allow that tone to come into your motion now, feel it flowing through your whole body. Imagine radiating that quality to others as well.

Walk in the world with that sense of yourself, full of vitality, clarity, and strength. Walk into your life with an open heart and mind. See with fresh eyes; hear with new ears; speak with a newfound voice.

Intention:

I release constriction and move into freedom and choice.

LIFE IS MOTION

Life is movement, change, and flow. Much as we might long for stillness, everything is always in flux, from the spinning of electrons and the spiraling of galaxies to the metabolism within our cells. Our bodies, emotions, and thoughts are in perpetual transition, always shifting from one state to another. Experience changes continually, because it is the nature of life to unfold. When you perceive life as movement, you can also appreciate yourself as part of the larger dancing reality of the cosmos.

Meditation is a great tool for getting used to movement on every level—currents of life force in the body, the rich flow of emotion, insights about ourselves and the world. We may not be able to control outer circumstances, but we can learn to stay anchored in our core and connected to our own inner flow.

By doing these practices at transitional moments, you are giving yourself the sense that you are always in movement—the experience of being centered and in your flow at the same time. You do not have to go to some other place to experience yourself. You do not have to hide away in a monastery. You can cultivate the quality of life you desire right where you are, in the midst of your life.

Chapter 4

AFTERNOON MEDITATIONS

AFTERNOON MEDITATIONS

The middle of the day is a time of ripening and fullness. The sun reaches its zenith in the sky, shining down upon all growing things with warmth and nourishment. The clarity of midday light gives courage to the heart and also illumines our subtlest flaws. Everything is exposed in Technicolor: Ah, this is the shape of my day; this is the shape of my life.

Afternoon is the midlife of the day. In its slow descent toward the horizon, the sun softens its gaze upon us, brushing the world with nuance and shadow. If we are fortunate enough to behold its setting, the artistic collaboration between sun and sky, we are gifted with poignancies of color and texture that reach right into the soul. No matter our age or the outer season, these waning hours of daylight speak to us of the autumn of life, the inevitable turn toward sleep and death. Nature reminds us that this slow turning can be rich with beauty, poetry, and grace.

In the afternoon, we can meditate on the fullness of life. In midafternoon, we can take a few minutes of conscious rest, honoring the natural rhythm that calls us to regenerate. Then through the rest of the day and evening, we can approach our activities well nourished and refreshed.

Feast Your Senses

You can do this awareness practice at lunch or whenever you sit down for a meal. Even the simplest fare, a cup of soup and bread, seems like a feast when you engage all your senses.

The midday meal is a prime time to practice gratitude for nature's abundance. At noon, the sun is high in the sky; the light is direct, shadows are few, and radiance surrounds our half of the world. The sounds of human and animal conversation resound in the air, and the dance of activity swirls around us. The fullness of life is evident, and when dining, we can make the most of that bounty.

Feasting in the evening has its own fullness, though it is more mellow, poignant, and nuanced. The sun is setting or has already disappeared; colors are subtler, light and shadow tease and entwine. The sensuality of an evening meal, taken alone or shared, can send us into reverie and rapture.

When you employ several sensory modes at once, they tend to enhance and amplify one another, contributing to even greater enjoyment. Your body is infused with information from different channels of pleasure.

Just taking a few seconds to breathe with awareness can revolutionize your experience of eating. When you pay attention, you can discover new tastes even in familiar food, you can be more satisfied with less quantity, and your instincts can guide you to eat for strength and health.

The "meditative taste challenge" is to take any of your preferred or usual foods and discover new ways to taste them. The adventure of eating is to taste and appreciate fully. Even if you're eating your favorite food, you may only pay attention to the taste for a second or two, maybe less. If you watch people in restaurants, you'll observe that most seem to notice what they're eating for only a moment, if at all, then ignore it or focus on talking.

It's as if there is a taboo against pleasure, and embarrassment about relishing food. Few people close their eyes and savor the aroma, flavor, and texture. You may feel self-conscious at first, but the rewards of taking pleasure are great—deeper satisfaction and better digestion and health. Soon you will be reveling in your senses with abandon.

Feast Your Senses Practice

When: *On your way to lunch or any meal, waiting for your food, and during your meal*

Where: *Anywhere you are eating*

Time: *Half a minute here and there*

If you are at work and heading for a restaurant or home, begin to switch into sensory awareness as soon as you leave your post. While getting in the elevator, meeting friends, walking down the street, scan all your senses.

The basic practice is to become aware of each sensory mode for the space of a few breaths: balance, hearing, vision, touch, smell, taste. Open your senses to the environment. Continue to cycle through these modalities from time to time throughout your meal.

Notice your breath as you move. Feel your feet, the sense of balance with each step, your shifting relationship to gravity.

Breathe with a heightened awareness of hearing the sounds of life around you. Listen to the nuances of sound.

Breathe with awareness of what you see. Take in the colors, forms, and movement.

Breathe with the sense of touch, the air on your skin, the drape of your clothes, the contact of your hands as they hold or touch something.

Breathe with awareness of smelling. Notice any odor or aroma in the air.

Breathe with the sense of taste, aware of sensations on your tongue.

You'll get so you can touch all of your senses in a few seconds. After all, you are always using your senses, even if only 1 percent.

When you sit down at the table, take in the atmosphere of this locale, whether it is your home, someone else's, or a restaurant. Appreciate it with all your senses.

Awaken your eyes to these surroundings. Notice the sense of space, the colors of the decor and people's clothing, and the movement as bodies flow through the room and gesture expressively. See yourself as part of this dance.

As you wait for food to arrive, awaken your ears to the ambient sounds in this environment. Listen to the murmur of voices, the bustle of activity, the melody from nature or a stereo, or the humming of machines. For a couple of breaths, focus on hearing the music of life. If you are with friends and conversing, listen to the music of their voices, and the meaning behind their words. Listen with your whole body.

Become aware of your body inhabiting space for one breath, then notice the shape of your form curving into the space around you. For another breath, sense your weight on the chair and the ground beneath your feet. Breathe consciously once or twice as you move to drink, eat, or communicate. Notice the expression of your face, the shift of your head, arms, and torso.

Become aware of touch for two or three breaths. Notice the texture of your clothes, napkin, and tablecloth. Feel the weight and temperature of the glass, cup, or silverware. If you're with a loved one, touch hands for an intimate breath.

Breathe in with the sense of smell, taking in any aromas from food cooked or served to those nearby. Let a breath or two whet your appetite and activate your digestive juices.

Wake up your tongue. Before eating, see if you can sneak in one minute of relaxing your tongue. While looking over the menu, listening to others, or simply waiting, pay attention to your tongue. Breathe in and out through your mouth a couple of times. The brush of air activates your tongue and alerts it to the delight to come.

When the food arrives, take a few breaths before eating to appreciate this culinary creation. Invent a sensual version of grace, being thankful for this gift of nourishment and beauty. Receive the colors of the food, and the plate or bowl. Take another deep breath, savoring the aromas.

With each bite, shamelessly enjoy the flavors and textures of your food. Experiment with discovering a new taste. The tastes on the front of your tongue, the middle, the back, the sides, the roof of your mouth, and the back of your throat will change with every second as you chew. Taste with the sides of your tongue. Breathe out, push some air over the back of your tongue, and notice the aftertaste—a very subtle pleasure.

Continue with your multisensory pleasure as you eat, taking a conscious breath or two with some modality whenever you like.

Finally, after you have partaken of this abundant deliciousness, pause for a moment to assimilate your experience before getting up to go. Breathe deeply with satisfaction and thanks. Absorb nourishment into your whole being. This appreciative pause aids your digestion on every level—body, mind, and soul.

Intention:

I open my senses to the richness of life.
I allow my body to be suffused with pleasure.

Mini-Siesta

Midafternoon is a natural time for a little siesta. If you have been on the go since early morning, you may feel an afternoon slump. As the sun dips toward the horizon, body energy takes a little dip as well.

Do you ever feel the call to slow down around three o'clock? You yawn, get sleepy, or maybe crave sugar? Your muscles start to get tense as you try to stay awake and fight off the fatigue? If you have a letdown in your energy, you are not alone. Most people have some kind of energy slump that follows the ultradian rhythm. What you need is an afternoon ultradian break or mini-siesta.

American culture generally does not honor the need for siesta; we think we should be outward, active, and continually productive like machines. Living things fluctuate, however, and are organized around cycles of action and rest. The rhythm of "now I'm feeling more active" and "now I'm slowing down" takes place every 90 to 120 minutes. Most offices do acknowledge these ultradian body cycles, providing coffee and lunch breaks at such transitional times. If you're at home, you have to create your own.

Workers are actually more productive and make fewer mistakes when they take ultradian breaks. You can think of ultradian rhythms as hour-and-a-half to two-hour waves of energy you ride. Then there is a pause that refreshes, and another wave sweeps you up.

It is weird to be in task mode, cranking work out, and all of a sudden, realize your mind is completely elsewhere. You find yourself fantasizing about an intimate relationship, a vacation, or the candy bars in the snack machine. You can personify the cravings and needs as visitations from your inner world: Sleepy, Hungry, Dopey, Horny, Teary, Grouchy, Dreamy, Spacey, Forgetful, and Oops (the one who makes mistakes). These are all signs that you need to take a break to let your energies rejuvenate.

We can always ignore an ultradian rhythm, force it aside and make ourselves work. But we pay a price—more stress hormones in our bloodstreams. The stress will catch up with us—somewhere, somehow—when we want to socialize, play, or rest. Sooner or later, we will have to pay off that debt.

If we cooperate with the call to slow down rather than resist it, we find that, paradoxically, we are quickly refreshed. Bringing awareness to the slumping movement helps to satisfy the inner need and allows us to make the most of the transition. We can give in, let ourselves rest, and then come back renewed.

Internal sensations, breath, and gravity are all your allies in this renewal. Sometimes five minutes is all it takes.

Mini-Siesta Practice

When: *Midafternoon*

Where: *At the office, at home, or anywhere*

Position: *If possible, lying down. If you are sitting, allow yourself to slump comfortably, or place your head on your desk or table.*

Time: *5 to 10 minutes*

This practice has three parts: Give In, Breath Release, and Eye Sweep.

In this meditation, you will enter the sensations of afternoon tiredness and give over to them completely for a few minutes. All you need to do is take a break from activity and turn your attention inward.

1. Give In. Become aware of your body. What sensations do you notice? Is there a desire to sink down, to let your shoulders slump? Slump describes the downward movement of fatigue, and it can feel as though you're being tugged toward the ground. It may even seem as if someone has pulled the plug and energy is draining through your feet. Gravity has a hold on you.

Get curious about this sensation, and open up to its possibilities. Giving yourself over to gravity can feel absolutely luscious and restful. Take the attitude that you don't have to hold yourself up; you don't have to be on duty right now or shape yourself for anyone. You can let go. Earth is right here beneath you, supporting you, holding you. Let yourself drift down, down into the support of the ground.

2. Breath Release. Become aware of exhaling. Long exhalations are relaxing, so with each breath, allow the exhale to lengthen. As you slowly let the air out, you relax more and more deeply. Emptying out, you let go.

After a few minutes, when you feel ready, become aware of the full cycle of the breath. Breathing connects you to the nourishing atmosphere of earth. With every inhalation, you draw in oxygen, nitrogen, and other elements given off by the plants of land and sea. With every exhalation, carbon dioxide is in turn cycled back as food for them.

Now begin to emphasize the inhalation. As you inhale, receive this life-giving substance we call air. Take it into your being, deeply. Experiment with the tempo of inhaling; speeding it up a bit can be very energizing. Inhalations are nourishing to every cell of your body. With every breath, you are being vitalized, fed, strengthened, and renewed. How do you sense this renewal?

Continue now, enjoying the full flow of your breath. Gradually include more awareness of your outer environment as you take in and give away each breath. Become aware of your location, noticing the sounds and other impressions around you.

Staying in touch with your inner sensations, begin to sit

up. Very gently begin to make a transition, slowly opening your eyes. Take several more breaths as you reorient yourself to the world.

3. Eye Sweep. Now, for another minute, activate your eyes. Notice your field of vision, the large circle or panorama in front of you. Begin to look at different points along its circumference, gently stretching your eyes up, down, side to side, and on the diagonals. Reach into the upper right quadrant, then sweep down to the lower left; up to the left and then down to the right. You'll feel your eye muscles being awakened and strengthened. Play with the movement, sweeping your eyes all around. Imagine you are sweeping the cobwebs out of your brain. To finish, close your eyes and place your palms over them soothingly for another few breaths. Then open your eyes gently and see the world afresh.

Intention:

I renew contact with myself and emerge refreshed.

Your Rhythms

Whenever you tune in to your body, the buzzing sensations of excitement and fatigue you feel are a consequence of the intersecting rhythms of nature: the hour and your cycle of activity, the day of the week, time of the month, and season. You might feel the need for a lunch break or walk, a night's sleep, a weekend to play, a monthly field trip, or your yearly vacation—all simultaneously. And at the same time, you may have the urge to get back to work or on to the next chore.

When you meditate, sometimes you will just feel peaceful, but more likely you will experience all of the cravings, desires, plans, and emotions in your body and mind. You may be flooded with thoughts. You may feel like a runner who takes a break to rub her sore calves. All of this is part of your natural rhythms. As you get into meditation, realize you don't need to judge anything, or censor any of your thoughts or feelings. Experience it all as the rhythm of life.

Wait Up

Many people spend half an hour, or more, of their day waiting in line. In the hustle of active lives, waiting can seem like a terrible waste of time—empty, unproductive, imprisoning. Our attitude itself creates stress: "I feel trapped. Let me outta here. This isn't my life." Maybe you look around, bristling. "Why don't those guys hurry up?" Some folks start pushing, and others just go numb.

People talk about killing time—which, if you think about it, is a strange concept—as if a moment's vibrant spaciousness must be stuffed and suffocated to death. This impatience with time appears to be a First World syndrome.

If you've ever traveled in the Third World, you have probably noticed people squatting and waiting for a bus. They may be there for hours, even days, but they are not postponing life. Life is there in that moment to enjoy. A community forms; jokes, stories, and cigarettes are shared. Waiting is a welcome relief from the drudgery.

Since waiting is a fact of life no matter where we live, we may as well make the most of it. Unexpected connections can occur, if we make ourselves available. Life is happening now, not just in our activities but in the moments in between them. In those gaps, we can loosen up our identities from the roles we play for others. We can simply be present, and let life surprise and teach us.

Meditative awareness enlivens perception and awakens us to new possibilities. Waiting can become an adventure of discovery that sparks creativity, opens the heart, and takes us into deeper appreciation of our humanity.

Many of the situations in which we find ourselves waiting are actually nexus points where the streams of human activity intersect. At an airport, for example, people from all over the world happen to convene at this particular place and time. Each traveler represents a wealth of experience—a culture, a family, a way of life. Each heart pulses with its private sorrows, joys, and dreams. Occasionally our eyes meet, a smile is exchanged, something of the soul is shared.

The next time you're at the airport, or sitting in the waiting room of your dentist, or standing in line at the post office or grocery store, play with the following awareness practice.

Wait Up Practice

When: *Any time you are in waiting mode*
Where: *In a lobby, airport, store, at the park, or as a passenger in a car, plane, or train*
Position: *Sitting or standing*
Time: *3 to 5 minutes*

First, orient yourself to the physical surroundings. Find a place that seems like your spot for now, somewhat like a dog circling before plunking down.

Notice your location, your body in this room, this building, and this part of the city. Within this larger context, you are simply present. You see the swirl of movement around you, you hear the sounds, but you are centered in yourself. You don't have to do or be anything special right now.

Sitting or standing comfortably, sense your own body. Notice what your breath feels like, the motion of inhaling and exhaling. With each breath you become more aware of yourself. Become aware of the outline of your body, the container of your skin, and the sense of being inside your own skin.

Now simply notice the ground beneath your feet. Feel your weight as you sit or stand. You are resting inside your skin, resting in gravity. Sink into the support of the ground. Here you are at this spot on the planet.

Say to yourself, "Breathing in, I'm refreshed. Breathing out, I'm relieved. I feel my skin. I feel my feet in contact with the ground."

Now, from this centered awareness, begin to open your attention to the people around you. Be curious, as if you are a writer or artist observing a slice of life, taking notes on the varieties of human experience. What can you observe?

Life has conspired to throw together this group of people for a few minutes—a revealing tableau of the human condition. In this moment, all these paths of life are intersecting, all these different tribes, cultures, subcultures. This is a chance to observe a subset of humanity, your humanity.

Within each person is a world of experience, a world of stories, a world of dreams. Within you is a world of experience, stories, and dreams. When you look around, what similarities of experience do you sense? What differences?

Life is here, now. Your life is here, now. Notice how people are relating, or not relating. Sometimes friendships form spontaneously, the way they do in a bar. Jokes are told, stories are shared, and philosophies of life are discussed.

Entertain the idea of making contact with someone. Just notice how you feel. Since you find yourself in the midst of all this, is there anyone you'd like to greet?

Now, staying in touch with yourself, gradually bridge back into action.

Intention:

My life is happening now, no matter where I am.
This moment is alive. I am present.

Road Peace

The roads of the world are like the blood vessels of humanity, pathways of circulation for fulfilling our needs and desires. Being in a car and going about our business is one of the major ways we interact with one another. This practice prepares you for a safe and enjoyable journey.

Most of us take for granted the freedom simply to head out the door, jump in the car, and zip anywhere we want, just because we want to. When this desire for unimpeded motion is not fulfilled, you may find yourself frustrated. Each delay or obstruction—waiting at the endless red light, being cut off by a rude driver, even having someone slow down in front of you to make a turn—may evoke a dramatic physical and emotional response of discomfort, irritation, or anger.

This is road rage, a symptom of stress. We all know how quickly our blood can boil and how dangerous that state of mind can be. Tension can breed an attitude of territoriality and entitlement: "Get out of my way, you jerk. I have more right to this space than you." The whole scene is a pressure cooker—volatile and ready to blow.

Driving is such a common activity that our cars have become almost like second homes. People shave, read the newspaper, eat, put on makeup, talk on the phone, sing, cry, surf the Internet, drink, and smoke cigarettes while they're behind the wheel. Driving is also potentially dangerous. Be aware that most people's minds are elsewhere while they are driving. Even drivers talking to passengers can be as impaired as if they were drunk, especially if it's an intense conversation. We all tend to forget that we are hurtling through space inside tons of metal and explosives (gasoline). Every year in the United States there are over six million car accidents, causing forty thousand deaths and millions of injuries. Researchers find that a significant percentage of accidents are caused by driver distraction or aggressive driving.

Getting angry because of typical traffic events can impair your driving skills, and the stress hormones your body releases take a huge toll on your health. Plus the irritation steals much of the pleasure out of the rest of your life. So it is really worthwhile to cultivate the attitude of Road Peace each time you get in the car, with the intention to travel serenely and safely to your destination. Doing so will positively influence your own experience as well as that of other drivers.

When you enter a car, you need to have your wits about you. This means your animal instincts are alert, your senses are wide open, and you feel relaxed and at ease. You can train yourself to be this way just by intending it, and by varying your behavior slightly.

Relaxed alertness will help you stay aware of other cars and the road, and be prepared for the unexpected.

There are many elements to cultivating Road Peace: breathing calmly, increasing sensory awareness, staying centered, maintaining a nonjudgmental spirit. Forgive other drivers in advance. In addition to being considerate to others by keeping proper space between cars and signaling when changing lanes, you can also send out thoughts of safety and communicate peaceful intent to those with whom you share the road.

Remember, you are in control of your own state of mind. Ultimately, no outer circumstance, no other driver, passenger, or pedestrian has the power to determine your experience. The power to live in joy and confidence resides within you. Claim that power by practicing peace, especially when you're on the road.

YOUR INNER HULK

Do you have a wild driving alter ego? Even the sweetest, most mild-mannered individuals may shift personalities when they get behind the wheel. Explore your road warrior persona—safely and consciously—before you get in the car.

A vehicle can be a place people act out their frustrations with life in general. If someone feels powerless at work or home, driving aggressively may give a sense of command. People with road rage are driving under the influence of the stress hormones in their bloodstreams. The Inner Hulk is threatening to seize control. Acting out violent impulses may make for entertaining movies, but on the road it can be disastrous.

Get to know your Inner Hulk. Along with its dangerous elements, this character will have useful qualities for you to assimilate. If aggression gives you a heightened degree of alertness, freedom, or empowerment, for example, learn how to access and exercise those feelings in other, safer ways.

Ironically, when you get enraged, you are in effect handing your power over to outer circumstances. As a rule, never drive when you're angry. Whenever you're obstructed, become alert, not angry. But if you find yourself possessed by rage while you're driving, pull over carefully and practice Road Peace. Taking these extra minutes to shift consciousness may save your life, the lives of the people in the car with you, and the lives of others on the road.

Road Peace Practice

When: *Before and during driving*

Where: *Outside or inside your car*

Time: *3 to 5 minutes*

Note: *Familiarize yourself with this practice before driving.* ***Do not use the CD when driving.*** *Listen to the CD in advance or pull off the road.*

If you can, leave early so that you do not feel rushed. Walk out the door two minutes before you think you need to, and give away that two minutes as a donation to world peace. In practice this means, if a signal is red, you can say, "Ah." If people in front of you slow down for a moment, you can give them that moment and not crowd them. By not hassling the drivers around you, you offer them a moment of peace.

Do a systems check before getting in the car. Just as a pilot does before taking off, walk around, check the tires, and make sure everything is in order.

Stand still for a few seconds, take a breath, and in your own way appreciate the fact that this car is available, that you have roads and fuel to use, and that you have somewhere to go. Just for a moment, stop taking all this for granted, and breathe in gratitude. In a few brief seconds, you can begin to gently transform your driving experience so that you become a more relaxed and alert driver.

When you get in the car, sit for a moment and imagine that your car is surrounded by a protective force field. Decree that nothing harmful can penetrate this shield of energy. Visualize your destination and the path you will be following to get there. Prepare to be around other commuters, and intend safety for everyone. Forgive other drivers in advance.

If you are religious, ask God to bless, or know that God is blessing, your vehicle, your route, and every person you come near. If you are not religious, you can say or think, "I intend peace to everyone on the road today," or simply take a breath with the word peace resonating in your mind.

As you put the key in the ignition, take another conscious breath, then start the car. Settle into the seat, and imagine the car as an extension of your body. Glance at the instrument panel as the car warms up for a few seconds, and then with your awareness scan your internal instrument panels. Be aware of your body as you sit in the seat, your muscles and nerves, and confirm that you are alert and good to go.

While driving, continually scan your senses. Like an animal awake to its environment, extend your awareness into the space around you, 360 degrees. Visually take in the whole situation, paying attention to the movement of traffic in the distance as well as close by. Activate your peripheral vision. Be aware not only of the area directly ahead but of the space behind you and to the sides.

Make a game of being alert and relaxed. Enjoy the feeling of composure, confidence, and centeredness within the flow of traffic. Imagine those qualities radiating from you and affecting your fellow drivers. To yourself and to them, communicate road peace.

If you encounter obstacles—flat tires, accidents, delays—consider them opportunities to wake up. Steer your emotions toward greater alertness. When traffic is crazy and people are driving badly, you can always pull over. Take a minute to check your tires, clean the windshield, and enjoy a few relaxing breaths while that unruly pack of cars goes by.

If you start getting angry, bring yourself back to reality. Remember the Big Picture. Talk to yourself, as if you are a coach giving instructions to a player. Say helpful things such as "Don't panic. You will still get there. You can afford to lose twenty seconds."

Mentally, remind yourself that you do not have to let the outer world determine your inner state. No one and nothing has power over your well-being. You have the ability to stay centered no matter what is going on. This is your life. This is your body. Your mental and physical health depend on this awareness.

If you still feel that your pressure cooker might explode, take some deep breaths, calming yourself until you can pull over. Once you are safely parked, begin to defuse your angry energy.

Unwind from your rage by taking a normal inhalation and holding your breath for a beat. Feel the oxygen filling you up, then exhale very slowly. Anger usually feels like heat, so find ways to cool off. Open the windows. Loosen your collar or belt. Take another deep breath, and let it out slowly. Continue doing this calming breath until the rage subsides. As you do, repeat out loud or internally, "I will not let road rage get the better of me. I will not allow anyone to control my mood. I claim the power of peace."

When you feel calm, take one big yawn, rub your eyes, and then reorient yourself to driving. Take a few more breaths, and become alert in all your senses. Carefully, pull back onto the road.

Intention:

***I travel through the world in peace and safety.
I communicate the power of peace to all around me.***

Chapter 5

EVENING MEDITATIONS

EVENING MEDITATIONS

In the transition between afternoon and evening, we harvest the fruits of the day and shift our attention toward relaxation and regeneration. An evening meditation helps us to unwind worktime pressures from our bodies, free our minds from obligation, and warm our hearts in solitude or social communion.

As night falls, our daylight persona falls away as well. In the privacy of home or the wildness of a party, we can let down, show other faces, express different selves, play and dream. There is an intimacy, sensuality, and soulfulness to the night, whether in quiet reverie, cozy snuggling, or raucous revelry.

The end of the day is a turning inward. The earth turns away from the sun, toward the coolness and darkness of space. We face the stars in all their glory, the gentle shimmer of moonlight, the depths of blackness in between. In a similar way, consciousness turns away from the glaring focus of day, to face the spaciousness of night.

Nighttime meditations center on letting go, releasing control, and forgiving ourselves and the world. Eventually we succumb completely, sinking into the healing arms of sleep.

Coming Home

When you come home, you cross the threshold from your workday, public life to your private sanctuary. As you enter your personal world, you can also come home to yourself and your body.

Too often, we bring the unfinished business and tensions from work or the outer world into our homes. This can be bad for your relationships, because if you come home carrying tension in your body and don't take time to release it, you are apt to "kick the cat"—take it out on someone else, or on yourself. So it can be useful to take some time to wash the day out of your hair.

Sometimes work is a refuge and home is a place of intensity. When you walk in the door, you might be faced with all kinds of new challenges. Your home may be noisy, a cauldron of chaos full of people. Or you may be returning to an empty house and an unpleasant sense of being alone. Either way, giving yourself time for a brief body scan can be a major blessing.

The Coming Home Body Scan is a method of quickly releasing tension and fatigue so that your evening, your after-work period, will be a happier, more relaxed experience. Take time to feel through all the movements from the day that are wiggling around in your nervous system; give them a chance to be sensed and released.

During a Body Scan, you tune in to background sensations—tiredness, frayed nerves, irritation, depletion, as well as any sense of pleasure. By paying attention to the physical impressions, you unwind the tensions left over from the day. You sense each area of your body, just paying attention to heat or cold, pressure and touch, tension or relaxation, tingling or vibration, aching or sweetness. Any area of the body can pick up tension during the day and will need to be tended and soothed.

As you get used to this process, you will be able to speed it up or slow it down to fit your schedule. You may even find you can start it before you walk in the door. You might observe revealing sensations as you get near your house or apartment. Stop, breathe, and give thanks. Cleanse yourself before you enter the sanctuary of your home.

This meditation can feel natural, as easy and unformed as taking a brief power nap. Or it can seem as intricate as listening to a band or orchestra. The body has many parts; you are a composite of numerous interrelated, highly cooperative organs, cells, and joints. When you listen to an area of the body as it vibrates with fatigue, you may hear a kind of music.

Coming Home Practice

When: *After you walk in the door. If possible, take a shower first.*

Where: *Someplace that feels like a sanctuary from the world*

Position: *Lying down, sitting upright, curled up somewhere, or even standing. Some people find it's easier to let go lying down. You might want to put a pillow under your knees and a cloth over your eyes. Have a blanket handy in case you get cold.*

Time: *5 to 10 minutes*

The Coming Home Body Scan has three phases: Settle In, Notice Background Sensations, and Head to Toe.

1. Settle In. For the first minute, just let yourself be. Give yourself time to settle in and make yourself comfortable. Whether you are lying down or sitting, begin to release your body weight to gravity.

Now make yourself available for whatever is calling your attention. You will probably have thoughts, images, and remembered conversations from the day floating through your mind. Allow this process, because it is your mind attempting to "clear its desk."

Breathe out with a whoosh or a sigh three times. This is often called a Cleansing Breath, because it seems to wash stress out of the system. You can continue doing it for several minutes if you like.

2. Notice Background Sensation. As you quiet down, shift your attention to the level of body sensations. At first doing this may seem unusual to you—what is a body sensation? But if you approach this practice casually, with a sense of curiosity, you will discover all sorts of tingling, pressures, pleasures, sensations of fatigue, delicious restfulness, and so on. This realm of sensing is as rich in its own way as music is to hearing and good food is to the sense of taste.

As you begin to relax, you may become aware of particular sensations calling you—aches, pains, tensions—that you did not have time to feel during your last action phase, the phase of working and commuting. Just let yourself be called to whatever is there for a minute.

3. Head to Toe. Now, simply become aware of your head. Feel around your crown, your scalp, the back of your skull. Notice the sense of your head resting on the floor, or on top of your spine. It may feel heavy or light.

Bring awareness to your forehead. Sense the curve of your brow, its shape, the skin. Notice the sensations around your eyes and behind your eyes. As you pay attention, any tension will tend to soften and release.

Now feel your nose and cheeks. Become aware of your mouth, lips, and tongue. If your jaw seems tight, you can slightly part your teeth. Sense your whole face.

Any of these areas, once you touch it with awareness, may call to you strongly. Some sensation or feeling will want attention.

If so, allow yourself to stay there for as long as it takes for your awareness to soothe that area. You may not get to the rest of your body. That's okay. Just keep showing up for yourself.

Whenever you are ready, proceed, scanning from the top of your head toward your toes. Notice the sensations in your throat and neck, which have been involved in speaking and holding up your head.

Bring awareness to your shoulders, your arms, and your hands. If you like, make a tiny, almost imperceptible shrugging motion with your shoulders, and notice how that subtly moves your arms and hands. Enjoy this marvelous interconnectedness.

Rest your awareness in your chest, your breasts, your heart, and feel the breath flowing within you. What sensations do you have in your chest? Warmth, pressure, tugging, vibration?

Again, in any of these areas, you may be called to pause and go deeper. If there is pleasure, bask in that feeling. If there is tightness, irritation, aching, or fatigue, allow that place to receive whatever attention it needs. Some part may want warmth, another, coolness. A part may crave space or want to be snugly held. In your imagination, give each part of your body exactly what it requests. Feel free to stay in each area as long as it takes for your awareness to bring balance and soothing.

When you are ready, proceed on to your belly. Be with the motion of the breath in your diaphragm. Notice whatever sensations are inside your belly and your lower back. Just be aware of any tightness or discomfort and also the pleasurable sensations of becoming more relaxed. Invite that place to soften, spread out, melt, whatever it needs.

Let your awareness come into your pelvis, your hips, and your buttocks. Give over to the sensation of gravity pulling you down into the earth.

Notice that there is an attraction between your body and the body of the earth. Gravity is a mysterious force of attraction and connection. Become interested in it. Gravity might be love, a love among all bodies. What does gravity feel like to you?

Now become aware of your thighs, your knees, your calves, your ankles, your feet and toes. Imagine or feel the flow of energy from your pelvis all the way down your legs. Notice if your right side is any different from your left.

Be with any place in your lower body that calls your attention. Dwell with whatever sensations are there.

Now gently scan your whole body. For the space of a few breaths, simply let your attention meander wherever it wants to go. All these sensations, tingles, and feelings are how life is touching you right now.

Some days you may find yourself lingering in one area, spending your whole time there, coming back to the sensations again and again. Anything you bring awareness to will tend to change, to melt or intensify as it receives what it needs. Certain problem areas will demand your attention, and you might be stumped as to what they want. Simply give them loving attention.

At some point, you will know that the process is complete

for the time being. When you are ready, take a few breaths, stretch gently, and yawn. Then get up to enjoy the rest of your day or evening.

Intention:

I give over to the regenerative power of conscious rest. I release the tensions of the day and am prepared to love and enjoy.

THE POWER OF REST

When we go to sleep at night, the body gradually shifts into more and more restfulness. One indication of rest is a reduction in oxygen consumption, because the body is doing less work. During sleep, over a period of four or five hours, oxygen consumption gradually decreases until it hits about an 8 percent reduction. When we wake up refreshed, it is because of this rest.

When we close our eyes to meditate, a different kind of rest response is triggered. We stay awake, yet over the next three to five minutes, oxygen consumption decreases 12 to 17 percent. This is not from any effort or intention on our part; it is something the body does when we give it permission to really rest.

So, paradoxically, meditative "conscious rest" is more powerful in some ways than sleep. How can this be? We think meditation is a way of triggering the healing, evolutionary instinct that is built in to the human body.

You don't have to be an advanced yogi to rest this deeply. It happens for beginners with just a few hours of training.

Party On

Party On is a practice to do before any social gathering—a dinner with loved ones, a party with strangers, or a holiday with family and friends. This is a meditation on acceptance of your many moods and inner parts, and compassion for the moods you sense in others. You can do this on your own, with a partner, or even in a group.

Human beings are instinctively social. We are raised in family groups, educated in groups, and usually work in groups. One of the challenges of being social animals is learning how to be true to ourselves when we are with others, for no one is a static, one-dimensional character. Inside every human being is an ever-changing theater of emotions, desires, attitudes, and moods.

The particular mix of these qualities is what makes you an individual. You may want to show only those you deem likable, but any group situation has a tendency to call forth all of who you are, even the facets you try to hide. For this reason, socializing can be nerve-wracking, relaxing, exhausting, exciting, heart-opening, scary, liberating, or fun.

Even the *thought* of going to a party can make you moody. Suddenly you're tired or cranky, or you get into a fight with your mate. Why does this happen? Moods feel weird, but actually they are clues to what you need. A mood represents a part of yourself you have been neglecting. When a mood comes up, your job is to be a good friend to yourself. Listen to the feeling for a bit; let it teach you something.

When accepted, every inner character, emotion, or mood gives you a gift of energy and balance. Each is an aspect of your humanity, a way of seeing and being in the world. Take a look at the expressions you admire, envy, fear, or scorn in others, and in yourself. You will identify with some qualities, and others you may reject. The disowned, shadow parts hold keys to your vitality, authenticity, and ultimately your intimacy with others.

For the sake of simplicity and usability, nothing beats the Seven Dwarfs as a typology of moods: Happy, Sleepy, Sneezy, Grumpy, Bashful, Dopey, and Doc. Toss in a couple more you find in the back of your mind—say, Lusty, Goofy, Defiant—and there you have a mood map.

When we let down our hair, we tend to swing to the opposite of our usual persona. For example, if all day you have been Doc—"on call" to deal with one crisis after another—on the way to a party you might find yourself Grumpy, Lusty, or Goofy. The mood comes up not to sabotage your life but to enrich your experience of yourself and balance you out.

This practice is a chance to let your opposing mood come to the fore to be felt, and to give you its gift of balance. Then when you are at the party, you will have more choice in what you want to express and how you want to express it.

Witnessing your inner characters leads to compassion for yourself, which is the basis of compassion for others. The more parts of yourself you can accept, the more you can just let yourself be when you are in social situations. The more comfortable you are with yourself and having a good time, the more you can let others do the same. You can let other people be different manifestations of the human animal.

Coming together socially can be seen as improvisational theater, a creative event with the potential for mutual inspiration. Every person contributes something to the whole. Get curious. Ask yourself, What quality will each person bring to the situation? What can I bring? What part do I play in this creation?

Party On Practice

When: *Before a party or family event*

Where: *Anywhere*

Time: *5 to 10 minutes*

This practice can be done with a partner or on your own.

In this practice you will be identifying and befriending parts of yourself—feelings you like as well as ones you have trouble accepting.

Sitting by yourself or with a partner, close your eyes and breathe out with a sigh a couple of times. Now take a moment to tune in to your mood. Do you have excitement or resistance about going to this event? What is your fantasy about what might happen? Breathe with whatever you notice—any images floating through your head, any feelings in your body.

If you were not to edit your feelings at all, which one would come to the surface? For example: I'm tired; I'd rather crawl into bed. I feel a little depressed. I am irritable and judgmental. Who wants to be around all those jerks anyway? I'm still angry about something that happened today. I have issues with someone at the party. I'm nervous, afraid I'll have to perform, be brilliant and clever. I'm excited about seeing my friends.

Now distill your mood into a simple phrase: I'm sad. I hate everybody. I'm pooped. I'm scared. I'm worried. I'm thrilled. Perhaps you feel like one of the Seven Dwarfs. I feel Grumpy. I'm Bashful. I'm Happy.

Now visualize the facial expression that goes with your phrase. You've seen this, in other people, and in movies or cartoons.

Outwardly express this phrase and the face that goes with it. Slowly open your eyes. If you are with a partner, you will need to take turns, so decide with a nonverbal signal which of you will go first. If you are by yourself, you will be your own witness, saying your phrase out loud.

When witnessing, it is important to maintain an open, nonjudgmental attitude. Be curious and welcoming. Don't comment or try to talk yourself or the other person out of the feeling. Think of this as improv. You can have fun with it!

Let the first person begin. Say your phrase once or twice and make the face that goes with it. Exaggerate the feeling. Let your body take on its posture. Be melodramatic, over the top.

Now, you who are witnessing: After your partner expresses, say the phrase back. If she says, "I'm sad," take a breath and then say, "You're sad."

Now silently switch roles.

If you like, do three rounds. You can find three different moods, or go deeper into one.

With each expression, consciously give acceptance to yourself, and to your partner. Remember: every feeling, every inner character, has a gift. See if you can sense the energy that is released.

When you have completed the witnessing, pause, take a

deep breath, and close your eyes again. Cover your face with your palms for several breaths. Simply feel.

Now make an opening gesture. Release your hands and sweep them forward and out wide. Open your eyes. Then relax your arms and take another moment to sit there quietly.

This simple awareness practice works wonders. You may surprise yourself with compassion and affection for all your inner parts. You may also be more compassionate toward others. Breathe with that feeling now. Let it flow between you and your partner, then to everyone you may be meeting.

Whatever you've been feeling, you can bet that others will be feeling it as well. The more familiar you are with your own process, the more understanding, compassion, and even humor you can have in this situation.

Now gradually begin to orient to action. Enter the world as you would a dream or a movie, with curiosity and willingness to explore. As you meet other characters, enjoy the creation. Ask, What aspect of human experience are they embodying? What part can I play, what quality of awareness can I bring to the situation? How can I set myself free to express what I know and love?

Make a decision to enjoy and experiment. Thank your partner, and yourself. Then take a few breaths and be on your way.

Intention:

I embrace all aspects of my experience. I engage with others with curiosity, acceptance, and creativity.

Heart Warming

In the course of a day, when do you have time to feel the emotional impact of your life? When do you have a chance to acknowledge your happiness, your loneliness, your bewilderment, grief, joy, bittersweet longing, homesickness for your country of birth, or just your need for a vacation?

A heart meditation is a time to dwell with everything that is in your heart. We all need a way to enter the world of feeling and warm ourselves at the inner fire. This is a good practice to do toward the end of the day. After the sun goes down in the outer world, we can tune in to the warmth and radiance within.

The physical heart is continually pulsating as it orchestrates the flow of blood throughout your body. The heart loves circulation, flow, rhythm, warmth, and oxygenation.

In addition to the physical heart, there is another dimension of the heart, a center of pure feeling. We talk about this function all the time in everyday language:

"He has a big heart."

"You are in my heart."

"Take heart."

"She's coldhearted."

"My heart sings at the thought of it."

"I have a broken heart."

"In your heart you know it's true."

The feeling heart is an organ of energy and perception. It keeps track of your relationship to the world. This heart vibrates, it sings, and there is a note for each of your major relationships.

Having an open heart means being available for the flow of life and love. It means being able both to give and to receive, and to be changed by the presence of another. Every one of us is designed to love, and to let our heart's energy flow inside ourselves and to others.

Nature created us to thrive in love, and as social beings we are meant to communicate and share. When life energy is circulating freely, we experience health, enthusiasm, courage, and joy. When the flow is obstructed for some reason, we have symptoms of pain, illness, ennui, or depression; we are sick in body or soul. Often we have learned to hold back; we've been hurt, or shamed, or had to freeze up our feelings in order to function. Icebergs are floating in the dark of the heart; occasionally a love boat hits one and sinks.

This meditation is about cultivating the sense of warmth and light in your heart, thus healing the cold and frozen places. You can do this practice a hundred times and every time have a different experience.

Heartwarming Practice

When: *Toward the end of the day*

Where: *Be in a cozy place. Light a candle, or settle yourself in front of a fire in your hearth.*

Position: *Sitting up or lying down*

Time: *10 to 20 minutes*

This meditation is time to breathe and pulsate with all that is in your heart, all of your love, your longing, and your warm memories.

Begin by thinking of someone or something you love *without reservation.* Notice the sensations in your heart as you remember your love. You may feel lightness, expansion, aching, or melting. You may feel joy or sorrow. Breathe with those feelings. Allow yourself to be with whatever is there.

When we love someone or something, we want to pay attention and we delight in paying attention. Attention, in essence, is love. Let your love teach you how to pay attention to the flow of life within you.

Now bring your hands to your heart. Rest your palms on your chest. You will feel a place that wants contact. As you breathe, you may notice a rising and falling motion under your hands, the soft flow of breath. Let your fingers and palms ride those gentle waves.

Feel the warm contact of your hands against your chest.

Imagine that warmth penetrating deep into your heart. You may feel your heartbeat.

The heart is designed to love, to express, to give and receive. Notice your longing to be in the presence of what you love. Let your heart be warmed by your love. Let the warmth melt any cold or frozen places, any part of you that is aching, afraid, grief-stricken, lonely, disappointed, or bitter. Let the flame of your love warm you from the inside.

Make a humming sound, such as "mmmm," "home," "huuum," or "ohhhhmmm." Keep saying it over and over, feeling how the sound vibrates your chest. In a casual, exploratory way, send the "hum" into your heart. Continue making the "hum," letting the sound become quieter, just a whisper. Gradually let it become an internal sound you are thinking or remembering. Then let the "hum" fade away, knowing you can return to it at any time.

Once again notice the contact of your hands on your heart. Slowly open your arms outward, as you would to embrace someone. Take a few breaths in this open-arm position, and then slowly, very gently, bring your hands back to your chest. You are returning to your heart, bringing that embrace into your own heart essence.

Repeat this movement several times with great leisure, as if you want to make the motion last as long as possible. This movement is an expression of the give and take of your love.

Sometimes we ache because we are not receiving enough love, and sometimes we ache because we are not giving enough love. This simple motion of in and out from the heart—opening to give and drawing in to receive—is a yoga of the heart, a way of expressing balance in giving and receiving.

Bring your hands back to your heart and pause. Simply breathe and savor the sensations. When you're ready, take another few breaths, open your eyes, and gently make the transition into your outer life.

Intention:

I am awake to love. I am ready to give and receive.
I am in the flow of love.

TUNE YOUR INSTRUMENT

Meditation is a time when you let the outer world take care of itself. There is an old saying, "Let the world turn without you." You *will* think about the outer world; that simply can't be helped. But take this chance to settle into yourself and get some R & R. You do not have to be on duty, so give yourself over to the inner processes.

When you meditate, you are tuning your instrument, your body and psyche. Each of us is a unique and sensitive instrument, with perceptions and creative responses unlike any other's. How you respond to the world is part of your individuality. Meditating lets you tune in to your brain and nervous system, and feel how life is vibrating through you. This practice allows you to fine-tune your senses to play in concert with the symphony of life.

When you meditate, you find your personal tuning fork, which is your sense of inner truth and life purpose. When you open your awareness, you will feel any places—your heart, your body, your nerves—that are out of tune. This can be painful, but when you pay attention, everything comes back into harmony.

Tune in to what's vibrating in your instrument. Then tune yourself to something you love, something that you are attracted to, something you feel in tune with, or would like to be in tune with. The meditation focus is a way of breathing and listening to the song of life, looking at the score, the notes on the page.

You have an inner musician or conductor. Meditation is a way of allowing her space and time to conduct you. She is your soul; she is your heart's desire. She is also attuned to the world, to the work that needs to be done in the world to make it a better place.

The forces of life and love are flowing through you at all times. Hear the vibration in your inner strings. Hear the song in your soul. Open your belly, your heart, your throat, and let your soul sing out.

Fall into Sleep

At the end of the day we lay our bodies down, close our eyes to the world, and fall into the night. We give up control and surrender to darkness. We need to sleep; it's a biological necessity. This need for rest reminds us, every day, that we are dependent on the healing rhythms of nature.

There are rhythms during sleep. Your body follows an ultradian rhythm of about ninety minutes, in which you sleep deeply for about eighty minutes, then dream for ten minutes. This goes on all night or for however long you sleep.

Sleep is a mini-death and a journey. Consciousness leaves the body and travels wherever it wants. Boundaries dissolve, and we become part of the universal body, the cosmos, the Great Unknown. The connection between sleep and death is a timeless mystery and the subject of much musing in all spiritual practices.

When we sleep, we enter the realm of the soul, the unconscious, the world of dreams. Anything can happen in the dreamworld. The soul is a wild adventurer, a trickster, a magician; we can see or be anybody, see or do surprising, even horrifying things. The improvisations of the unconscious are inspiring and utterly humbling, exposing our deepest desires, urges, and fears.

Falling asleep can be a profound meditation on letting go. We can learn to appreciate not only the exquisite relaxation of falling asleep but also the deep relief of releasing our daytime selves. We let go of activity, we let go of our persona, our body identity, the particulars of our lives, and all the ways we are localized in time and place. Freed from the container of the skin, consciousness melts into eternity and spreads into infinity for a few hours. We die to the world, drift and dream. Then in the morning we somehow make our way back, condensing into this body, this time, this family, this spot on Earth, this life.

When we fall asleep, we can give ourselves something wonderful to fall into; we can fall into love. The depth of meditation comes from letting yourself be with something you love, then falling into the experience. When we fall asleep, we fall in anyway, so we may as well succumb to what we love.

Many spiritual teachings describe the state beyond death as love itself, the divine force that connects everything in the universe. When we let go of identity, let go of thought, let go of life as we know it, we are left with the essence of love. Discovering what that feels like for you can be tremendously transformative.

Preparing for sleep can be a prayer, a blessing, a peace offering to the unknown. We forgive everything and everyone. We forgive ourselves. We surrender to love.

Fall into Sleep Practice

When: *Preparing to sleep at night*

Where: *Lying in bed*

Position: *Place yourself in the most comfortable position possible. You might want to use extra pillows under your knees, or curl around a body pillow if you prefer lying on your side.*

Time: *5 to 10 minutes*

There are three parts to this meditation: Review and Release, Get Cozy, and Fall into Love.

As you fall asleep, develop the sense that you are falling into a rich and wonderful inner world, the world of your dreams. Since you are going to be dreaming anyway, you may as well set the stage!

1. Review and Release. Before sleeping, it is helpful to release the day. Take several minutes to review the movement of your day, play by play. Take stock of your actions and interactions, and assess their consequences. Savor the texture of your life. Remember the moments of pleasure and satisfaction. Feel any moments of discomfort or difficulty. Acknowledge the lessons life is throwing your way, and how you want to be more aware in those situations. Breathe with whatever insights you have.

Then, *let go* of the day. Release everything. Forgive everything and everyone. Bless everybody you know and let them go for now. Forgive yourself completely. Let everything fall away.

2. Get Cozy. Prepare to fall into sleep. You can fall with all your senses. Start with the literal sensations, or how you feel right now.

Make your bed a comforting nest. Plump up your pillows, adjust the blanket, and make yourself cozy and safe. Nestle into your favorite position, and give yourself over to the sense of your body relaxing and settling down.

Experience with all your senses the feelings and sensations of being cozy: the sweetness of fatigue calling you to rest, the comfort of snuggling into your covers, the softness of gravity pulling you down into the mattress. Be aware of the flow of your breath, the quiet sound of your own breathing. Sigh or yawn, if you like, exhaling deeply.

3. Fall into Love. Now begin to tune yourself to what you love about the universe. Choose an image that gives you a sense of connectedness, sanctuary, inspiration, or deep pleasure. It might be an aspect of nature—a mountain, desert, forest, lake, or beach. You do not have to visualize the entire area. Just notice a smell, a color, a texture, a sound, or a motion that you particularly enjoy.

Let your imagination take flight. You might visualize the earth as if seeing our beautiful blue planet from space. Or enjoy the sense of merging with the night sky, the shimmering of stars and rich black space. Expand into the universe. Let your body dissolve into the substance of space.

Your love may be the feeling in your heart for someone you know, or for a beloved pet. It may be the sense of being held by a loving presence, by God, by the Divine Mother, or by the universe. Imagine loving arms wrapped around you, embracing you fully, unconditionally.

Be with your image and feeling, however you experience it. Immerse yourself in the image completely; be right there. Become one with the image and sensations. Give over to the warmth, tenderness, and expansiveness of love. Let the knowledge of love suffuse your whole being.

Release your body completely to the healing power of the night. When we fall asleep, we let go of ordinary reality and surrender to the mystery of sleep and dream. We float and drift beyond this world.

Float in the warm ocean of love. Be held by love, supported by love, surrounded by love, and permeated by love. Let your body go, melting into love, breathing love, and becoming love. Falling, falling now, into the depths of love, falling into healing sleep, fall into dream.

Intention:

I will awaken gently just before the alarm.
I will wake up naturally, happy about the day ahead.

Still of the Night

Lying in bed in the quiet of the night can be pleasurable and fascinating. Most everyone around us is asleep, fewer motors are running, a sweet darkness is blanketing the world. There is a fecundity and mystery to the world of night. The glaring light of daytime consciousness surrenders to the dreamy reflections of moonlight and stars.

Sometimes during the night thoughts and emotions that we don't have space to feel during the day can surface, either in our dreams or by waking us up. Freed from the focus of daytime activity, these revelations break through into nighttime consciousness, often giving us information crucial to our health, our relationships, or our career. Sometimes the insights spark our intuition.

When you wake up in the wee hours, what do you do? Fret? Toss and turn? Or sink deeper into the experience of the moment? The mind may be racing with unfinished business, projects, and cares. In the quiet of the night you might do some of your best thinking—recalling important details, or being inspired by some creative revelation. Or you might tense up, sure that in the morning you won't have the energy needed for the day.

Here's a great alternative. For this meditation, stay snug in bed, lying in whatever is your most comfortable and comforting position. The point is to be immersed in the subtle, peaceful sensations of resting. By staying physically at rest and mentally tuned to relaxation, your body is regenerating deeply even if you're awake. Quite likely, you will let go so much you will soon drift off into sleep.

Still of the Night Practice

When: *In the middle of the night*

Where: *Lying in bed*

Position: *Place yourself in the most comfortable position possible. You might want to use extra pillows under your knees, or curl around a body pillow if you prefer lying on your side.*

Time: *5 to 10 minutes*

When you awaken in the middle of the night, instead of getting up, bring your attention to the sensory world. Begin by scanning for comfort and pleasure. What can you find that is pleasurable?

If you enjoy the quietude and darkness, become even more aware of that experience. The sounds, or absence of sound, in your environment can be soothing. The darkness can be rich and velvety, surrounding you like a thick and fluffy comforter. Silence can be a symphony of inner sounds, exquisitely subtle and entrancing. Sink into your experience of the night.

ANXIOUS NIGHT

Note: *If the night evokes fear or anxiety for you, you can be with yourself in two ways. You can provide an antidote by focusing on other pleasurable sensations as in the Still* *of the Night practice. You can also acknowledge the fear and enter it with awareness, as is described here.*

Fear often seems like an unwanted stimulation. It can be sensed as a vibration permeating the body or some part of the body, a tremulousness or excitement. Feel this excitation, with openness to finding good in it.

Is the anxiety waking you up for a reason? If you examine the content of your anxious thoughts, they may clue you in to something important. Are you neglecting some part of yourself, or one of your children, your marriage, your career, or your body? Have you lost someone and not made time to grieve? Or have many great things happened and you haven't made time to bask in gratitude? If the fear that wakes you up is a phone call from your deep self, what is the message?

Breathe deeply, accepting the thoughts and feelings. Receive the message, and tell your psyche that you are paying attention to its gift. Commit to taking some time tomorrow to reflect upon its meaning.

Release the thoughts for now. They may still come and go, but give them lots of room. Instead of holding them tightly inside your head, envision them floating out into the vastness of space. Then shift your attention to the sensory practice of Still of the Night.

Imagine that you are enveloped in a peaceful, loving atmosphere. Become aware of pleasurable sensations. Notice the texture of the sheets, the soothing weight of the covers, the cushiness of your pillow. Nestle into that cocoon of comfort, softness, and warmth.

Be aware of your body weight supported by the bed. Allow yourself to sink further into that support. Feel how every muscle falls loosely off your bones, relaxing into gravity. How heavy can you be? Release any sense of holding yourself up.

Sense the skin on your back, and imagine it spreading and melting. Feel the muscles widening and softening. The whole back of your body is dissolving and opening. Your spine floats, drifting down into the mattress.

Now gently bring your attention to your face and head. Let your head be supremely heavy. Feel your scalp and the skin on your forehead smoothing out. Sense your eyes falling back into your skull. Soften the place right in front of each ear and let your jaw release. Relax your lips and tongue, and slightly separate your teeth.

Now notice the rhythmic flow of your breath, gentle waves of inhalation and exhalation. What does your breathing feel like? Become curious about the exhale. How long does the breath flow out? Empty yourself a little more with each exhalation.

With each breath, let go, emptying, dissolving, and releasing. The sensations are delicious. Your back is spreading wide; your face is melting soft. Your whole body is relaxing deeply, becoming heavier, sinking toward the earth. As your body sinks down, your spirit drifts freely up and away.

Intention:

I rest in the comfort of the night.

Chapter 6

MEDITATION TIPS

MEDITATION TIPS

The 1 Percent Solution

The benefits of meditation transform your sense of self and how you relate to the world. You will notice small, almost imperceptible enhancements in how you handle your thoughts and emotions, and how you see and feel other people.

Get used to meditation a little at a time. Be gentle and patient with yourself. You have to give your nervous system and senses time to change, test, fine-tune, balance, and integrate. If you don't feel like meditating some days, don't be concerned. Come back to meditation another day or use a different technique.

It would be a lot to change 1 percent in a month. That would mean changing 12 percent in a year, and no one does that except in the most extreme circumstances. But 1 percent is a good approximation to think about, because in a day it's just barely noticeable. And that's what you want—just barely noticeable benefits. Those are the ones that become permanent parts of your life.

Our perceptions can be changed in a moment, but stabilizing ourselves in that more awakened state is a great challenge and requires persistent attention and cultivation.

Small doses of meditation throughout the day are good, because tiny changes are easier to integrate. Strange as it may seem, inner peace is a very difficult state to integrate. *All* the benefits of meditation are challenging to integrate. This is because meditation intensifies your senses. It does not just give you a little relaxation—it gives your body a chance to begin to retune all your reflexes and reactions. You develop more choice about when to be relaxed and when to feel tense.

Making very tiny changes, then giving your body a chance to get used to them, is the way to go. That is why a minute here, five minutes there, a few minutes yet another time, going at your own pace, is best.

Bad News, Good News

The bad news about relaxation is, you can't relax without letting go of tension. This sounds simple, but what it means in practice is that as you relax, you will become aware of sensations of tension release in your muscles and nerves. You can feel yourself unwinding, and unwinding always hurts a little. As you relax, you often remember what you were tense about.

So there you are, meditating along and having a good time; then suddenly your mind is filled with images, thoughts, conversations, and sensations pertaining to some unfinished business or unresolved conflict. Perhaps you feel a throb of heartache or grief over something that happened in the past.

The good news is that this process is natural and beneficial. Meditation is a rest state, a healing state, so whatever within you needs healing will come to the forefront to be healed. This same process happens when you are asleep and dreaming, but since you are unconscious then you can't complain too much.

In meditation, since you are awake, you can either cooperate or interfere with your own healing. There is much to learn from this debriefing, therapeutic process of stress release. If you do not understand this cycle of relaxation and release, you will tend to resist it.

And if you start resisting, then you are no longer meditating—you're just resisting.

Sometimes what you experience will show you that you need more support, and more skills. In that case, seek out a counselor, therapist, mentor, coach, priest, rabbi, or teacher whom you trust.

A Million Thoughts

Most of the time, people meditate just fine, but they think they have failed because their minds aren't blank.

You *think* you have failed when you go back and forth between relaxation and being aware of tension.

You *think* you have failed when emotions come up. You *think* you have failed when you get teary or excited.

You *think* you have failed when you spend the whole meditation time musing about someone you love.

The Truth:

You can have a million thoughts and still be meditating. Your body is practicing not flinching when you think of the stuff that bugs you. You will always alternate between tension and relaxation. That's how the bodymind works to heal and repair.

Your emotions come up because you have given yourself a safe time and place to feel. Thinking of someone you love is great. This is your quiet time, when you have the privacy to touch the depths of your heart. Let whatever you find there be your focus for the moment.

Wash the Fear out of Your System

During meditation, one of the main things the bodymind does is to wash the fear out of your system. It does this by going into relaxation and, while in this easy state, bringing up each fear, reviewing it, and saying, Hmm, do I really need to be worked up about this? The process happens automatically, and you can't stop it. This is why when you get relaxed in meditation, you will start thinking about all the issues of your life.

Anxieties, insecurities, and stresses accumulate in your nervous system and muscles, and keep you locked in the past. They obscure the real challenges of your present life. Meditating helps you to clean the slate so that you can respond to life, your life in the present, more quickly and clearly, with access to your inner resources.

As you release the fear from your nerves, you will be more able to experience joy. These meditations are about appreciating small moments, which will keep you in practice. You will notice more detail in your surroundings, more novelty, delight, and surprise.

On Your Way

In this book, we have described a variety of transitional moments that can serve as gateways to meditation. Be on the lookout for your own special moments, the ones so private you don't tell anyone about them. There are things you love and have cultivated the art of paying attention to: a candlelight bath, those delicious breaths you take at the end of a run, a certain way of listening to music, gazing at the ripple of a stream when you are fly-fishing. These are all ways of being with the natural elements of water, earth, light, or air and are incredibly renewing.

Adapt, improvise, and embellish the theme of these awareness practices. Find your own way. Tending to your own needs enriches your ability to be with others. You'll discover that even a few seconds of heightened attention can enlighten your experience throughout the day.

Meditation, alluring as it is, is not an end in itself. The purpose of meditation is to help you learn how to love, work, play, and rest. You will be able to notice how well you are doing in meditation by tiny, gradual enhancements in the ways you function in all these arenas.

As you become more open and perceptive, the world will seem more welcoming and friendly. You will see magic doorways everywhere, possibilities for enjoyment and connection. You will have more to give, and be more generous and forgiving. Your increased ability simply to pay attention in quiet moments will strengthen the bonds of intimacy with those you love. This is because meditation is actually the practice of becoming more intimate with life.

We wish you many magical moments.

Acknowledgments

The approach to meditation we are describing here is inspired by an early Sanskrit text, the Vijnana Bhairava Tantra. Lorin has a version of this, "The Radiance Sutras," on his Web site, www.lorinroche.com. An academic version of the Bhairava Tantra has been published by SUNY Press with the superb title *The Yoga of Delight, Wonder, and Astonishment,* by Jaideva Singh, with a foreword by Paul Muller-Ortega.

Recently we found an eloquent description of the hours of the day in the poet David Whyte's *Crossing the Unknown Sea: Work as a Pilgrimage of Identity*—a synchronistic discovery and encouragement on our subject. We recommend this book to anyone wanting to bring more soul into her or his work.

To Charles Bernstein flows immense gratitude for composing such elegant music for the CD. Our creative collaboration is a true joy. We give thanks to our agent, the marvelous Gareth Esersky from the Carol Mann Agency, for our deepening association. Much appreciation to Jean Lucas, our mighty editor, who called this book into being and delighted us with tales of her triathlon adventures in between editorial notes.

We thank all of our teachers, for passing on their wisdom and alerting us to this marvelous way of appreciating life, and those who study with us, for continually enriching our understanding.

Above and below all, we bow in gratefulness to the one who set this world in motion.

About the Authors

Camille Maurine and Lorin Roche are married and are the authors of *Meditation Secrets for Women: Discovering Your Passion, Pleasure, and Inner Peace.* Dr. Roche is also the author of *Meditation Made Easy, Whole Body Meditations*, and *Breath Taking*.

Camille Maurine was trained in dance, theater, and the healing arts. Her work, kinAesthetics, is a fusion of movement, yoga, meditation, and expression. She is the creator of Moving Theater, a transformative performance process. Camille gives workshops and private instruction at the Continuum Studio in Santa Monica, California, and travels to teach and perform.

Lorin Roche has been teaching meditation since 1968 and holds a Ph.D. from the University of California. In the mid-1970s, Lorin began developing Instinctive Meditation, a way of meditating that feels like an innate skill you are remembering rather than a technique imposed from the outside. He works by phone, e-mail, and in person with meditators of all traditions all over the world.

Lorin and Camille live in Marina del Rey, California, and travel together to teach. You can reach them through their Web sites: www.lorinroche.com and camillemaurine.com.

Charles Bernstein (www.charlesbernstein.com) is an award-winning composer, author, and teacher who has written music for over a hundred films and whose book *Film Music and Everything Else* has won praise from critics and musical colleagues. His world-beat CD, *MASS: Voices of the World,* explores rhythmic spirituality in various cultures. This is his first collaboration with the authors of *Meditation 24/7.*